Knitted
SHAWLS

Knitted
SHAWLS

25 RELAXING WRAPS,
COWLS AND SHAWLS

CHRISTINE BOGGIS

CONTENTS

Sunshine Shawlette 54

Love Triangle Shawl 58

Skyfall Shawl 78

Bundled Cowl 82

Journey Shawl 84

Wedding Wrap 100

Shades of Grey Shawl 116

Harvest Home Cowl 122

Cuddle Wrap 128

INTRODUCTION

I've been knitting since I was a teenager, but I didn't knit my first shawl until I became the editor of the UK-based monthly hand-knitting magazine *Knitting*. I'd never worn a triangle shawl in my life; the closest thing I ever had was fabric pashminas or wraps – and they were only worn to balls, black-tie events or as scarf alternatives.

One of the first things I noticed when I joined *Knitting* was the shawls. Shawls on Ravelry, on Instagram, on Pinterest, in books and, of course, in magazines. Simple shawls, complex shawls, shawls where I had absolutely no idea how they could possibly have been constructed. I loved the look of them, the cosiness of a giant wrap you snuggle into like a blanket, the elegance of lace draped over shoulders, the cool of a triangle shawl worn bandana-style, and the practicality of a simple cowl. As a knitter they intrigued me – just how did they work? Sometimes I could be halfway through knitting a design and I still didn't know. But perhaps the best thing about a hand-knitted shawl is what it says about the wearer, which is one of two things: either 'I am a knitter' or 'a knitter loves me'.

Because knitting shawls is a commitment. OK, knitting anything is a commitment, but these are no chunky hats or simple mittens, they're not even a pair of socks you could dash off in a week or two. Shawls are major projects you want to love knitting as well as wearing. You need to love working on them, and then you can spread that joy, warmth and affection to someone you love – or to yourself as you wrap up in the comfort of your own creation.

That is what this book is all about. These are shawls designed to be delightful to knit. Whether you start with a few stitches you can count on your fingers or with a long row, they offer plenty of relaxing, straightforward knitting, perfect for meditation or as an accompaniment to TV, radio or audio books. But they are also designed to interest and intrigue, with new techniques to learn and moments when you will need to concentrate on nothing but your knitting – a great way to bring yourself fully into the present moment.

WHY KNIT SHAWLS TO RELAX?

Many knitters take up their hobby to help them calm, de-stress and decompress. I started knitting because I wanted to make unique clothes and accessories that I couldn't find in shops, but I got really hooked on it when I had a stressful job with an international news agency and would find that after my shifts had ended I was mentally and physically exhausted but too wired to sit still. Knitting gave me something to occupy my hands, which allowed me to relax enough to focus on some really good TV, and the combination helped me wind down from the anxiety of the day's work. Knitting scarves and sweaters for my friends and my then boyfriend, now my husband – all of whom, at that time, were at the opposite end of Europe from me – helped me to feel connected and close to them, even though I was far away, which was a great comfort at a lonely time in my life. Since then, I have knitted my way through several bouts of depression, including two lots of post-natal depression, and plenty of anxiety; I find it always helps.

But there can be stressful things about knitting. For example, if you have spent a lot of money on yarn and it's not coming out the way you expected it to, or if it doesn't look like it will fit right. If you've got any issues with your own body shape (and let's face it, who hasn't?) there is the anxiety that the garment won't look the same on you as it does on the model. And then there's swatching (see page 11). Some people love it, others hate it and just won't do it.

Shawls take all this stress out of the equation. A shawl will look pretty much the same on you as it does on the model, whatever your size or shape. If you choose an alternative yarn and it comes out a different size or shape to the sample, chances are it will still be something you can wrap around your neck or shoulders. If you hate swatching, don't bother – just go for it. The result might not be exactly what you see in the picture, but it might be just as great. Just go with the flow and enjoy yourself.

HOW TO USE THIS BOOK

This book is designed as a step-by-step guide for absolute
beginners as well as a design collection for crafters at all
levels. You can work your way through it one project at a time,
from a simple slipknot to complex brioche stitch, learning
a wide range of the most popular knitting skills along the way.
For each technique you learn there is a shawl, wrap or cowl
you can knit to practise and perfect your new skill.

Alternatively, you can use this book as you would any
knitting publication, picking out the projects you fancy
and working on them in the order you choose. Each project
lists the techniques used and where to find them in the
book. So what are you waiting for?

TOOLS **OF THE TRADE**

*The great thing about learning to knit is that all you need are sticks and string –
it's the perfect post-apocalypse life skill. However, as I'm writing this pre-apocalypse,
there are a few great tools you may want to invest in.*

NEEDLES

The traditional knitting needle is a straight needle (2), basically a stick with a point at one end and a bobble at the other. These are great for basic flat knits but aren't ideal for most of the projects in this book, simply because they are less versatile and spacious than circular needles. However, some knitters just don't like circular needles, so there are a number of projects you could knit on straight needles if you're really careful. If the project just says it requires needles, you can give it a go on straights. If you can't work the techniques on straight needles the project will specify a circular.

Circular needles (3) are best for shawl knitting because they can accommodate the very large numbers of stitches many of these projects involve, and they also take the weight of the project off your wrists and let it sit in your lap. They are essential for techniques such as knitting in the round, diluted garter stitch and two-colour brioche. They come in two options: fixed needles and interchangeable sets. Fixed needles are great for one-off projects, but if you like knitting with circular needles it could be worth investing in an interchangeable set, which come with a number of different-sized tips and different-length cables, so you can use them for all sorts of projects.

Needles come in a number of different materials – bamboo, aluminium and plastic are popular, but you can also get them in carbon fibre, walnut and even solid silver. Wooden needles are lightweight, warm to the touch and less slippery than metal ones so they can be comforting if you are worried about your stitches getting away from you. On the other hand, metal could work better if you are a tight knitter and need something to help your stitches slide. I prefer both of these to plastic, which I find a bit sticky and inflexible, but wood is my favourite material to work with. I like to try out lots of different needles and my favourites are always changing.

OTHER TOOLS AND ACCESSORIES

Stitch markers are essential when it comes to knitting shawls – placing markers at strategic points means you can work your increases and patterns at certain points without having to count all your stitches. This is crucial to making the shawl knitting experience a relaxing one (unless you just love counting stitches). There are three types of stitch markers you can use. One is a simple ring (6) that slips on to a needle in between stitches to mark a certain point in the knitting. This doesn't need to be something expensive – you could just make a loop from a small piece of scrap yarn. The second is a locking or opening stitch marker (7) that looks like a tiny safety pin. This can be used just like the ring markers, or placed in a stitch to mark a certain point in the knitting. Again, you could use an ordinary safety pin, although this might be a bit cumbersome. The third is a split ring marker (8), which can be used like a locking marker, but doesn't lock.

You will also need a measuring tape (1), good scissors (4), yarn or tapestry needles for weaving in ends (5), and for some of the projects in this book you will need a basic sewing kit.

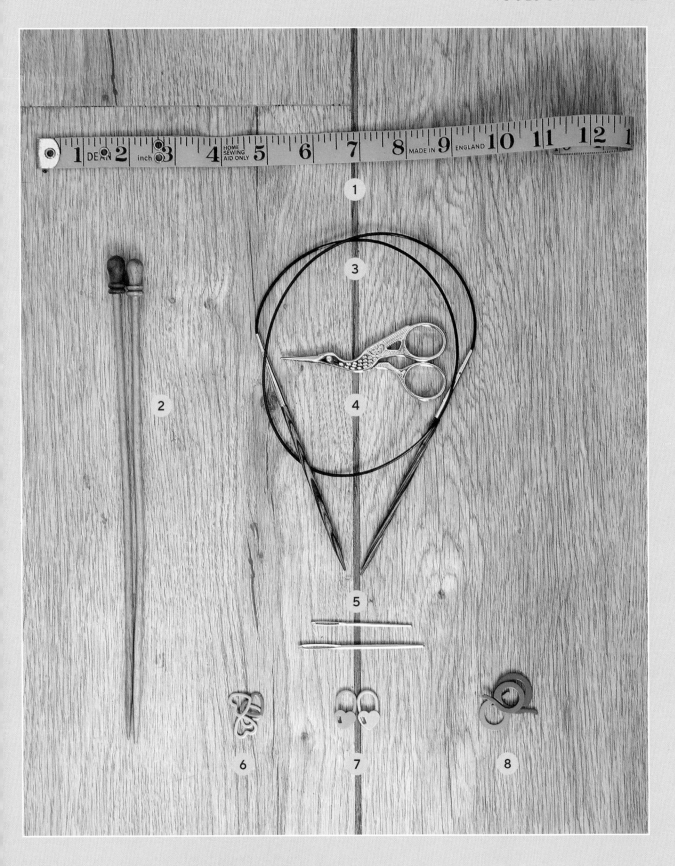

YARNS **TO LOVE**

The designs in this book use a wonderful array of fibres that are fantastic to work with.

The fibre you'll see most is wool. The projects use all kinds of wool, from super-soft Merino to deliciously crunchy rare British breeds, and everything in between. If a wool has been superwash treated it means it has been treated with chemicals to make it machine-washable.

Other fabulous fibres in these designs include alpaca, which comes from the eponymous camelids. It is one of the softest and warmest fibres you can knit with – and Suri alpaca is even softer and more lustrous than other types. You will also find cashmere – a soft, luxury fibre that is combed from the underbellies of cashmere goats; mohair, which comes from angora goats; cotton – a fibre spun from the cotton plant; and silk – a protein fibre derived from silkworm cocoons. Lastly, there are acrylic and nylon, which are synthetic fibres made from chemicals that are derived from petroleum and coal. Stellina is a metallic nylon fibre that adds shimmer and sparkle to a yarn.

MAKING IT **YOUR WAY**

How can you adapt designs to your own style and favourite yarn?

You may find you like a shawl in this book but don't like the yarn it's knitted in. Perhaps you've got a yarn in your stash that you're desperate to work with, and one of these patterns is its perfect partner. Shawls are great projects for yarn substitution because they don't need to fit too precisely, and with some of the designs – for example, *Easy Does It Capelet* (see page 24), *Mountain Shawl* (see page 34), *In-flight Shawl* (see page 52) and *Journey Shawl* (see page 84) – can be adapted quite straightforwardly to a different yarn.

Start by swatching. Look at the ball band of your chosen yarn to find the recommended needle size and number of stitches to 4in (10cm) and cast on double that number of stitches, then knit double the number of rows given for 4in (10cm), to get what should be an 8in (20cm) square. As well as giving you

plenty of fabric to measure your own tension, this square will tell you if you're happy with the recommended needle size, and it's also a good idea to wash and dry the square to see how your finished project will launder.

If your tension matches the given tension in the project, make sure you have enough yarn (check the length given rather than the yarn weight, as it is a better measure) and you're good to go.

If your tension doesn't match the given tension, you will need to do a few calculations. For a rectangular project like the *Easy Does It Capelet*, you will need to use your tension swatch to work out how many stitches to cast on. For example, if your yarn gives you 20 sts to 4in (10cm), you will need to cast on 80 sts to get the width of approximately 16in (40cm) of the sample capelet. Then simply knit until your capelet is as long as the one in the book, and choose buttons that will fit through your stitch holes.

If you're knitting a project that starts with a garter tab, make sure you've got enough yarn to complete the project – again, based on length rather than yarn weight – then cast on and give it a go. You may have to knit more or fewer rows to get to the length and width you want, but in general the method will be very similar. When you've reached the length you want, move on to the edging instructions.

Please note that if you change yarns, even to another yarn with the same tension as the pictured shawl, your project is likely to look quite different from the one in the book. Not just colour and texture but shape are very dependent on the interplay of fibre, tension and needles, so don't substitute a yarn unless you're happy to have some unexpected results.

Also, some projects will not lend themselves to yarn substitutions. Cowls, for example, need to fit a neck in a certain way, and if you're thinking of using a different yarn for a kite shawl, please make sure you have plenty of yarn, as these aren't projects you can easily cast off early.

ABSOLUTE BEGINNERS

MAKE YOUR VERY FIRST STITCHES AND TURN THEM INTO SHAWLS

'Really, all you need to become a good knitter are wool, needles, hands, and slightly below-average intelligence. Of course superior intelligence, such as yours and mine, is an advantage.'

ELIZABETH ZIMMERMANN

KNIT TO MAKE YOU
FEEL GOOD

Whether it's about making the stitches or finishing a project,
knitting helps you relax and feel better.

Knitters half-jokingly divide themselves into two camps: product knitters and process knitters. Product knitters are those who romp avidly through their projects, all the time dreaming of the day they can wear the finished knit or see the look on a loved one's face when they give it as a gift. Process knitters are the ones who will cast on with nothing particular in mind, simply for the love of knitting itself.

Really we've all got bits of both sides in us. For a long time I was very much a product knitter, buying yarn for individual projects and working away at them until they were done, either to be given as gifts or worn to an event. But I wasn't all product knitter – if I had just wanted a finished garment I could have gone out and bought it.

Now I consider myself very much a process knitter. As a designer and knitting writer I have a ridiculous stash and will cast on projects on a whim, just to see how the yarn feels or how a particular technique works, and then leave them lying fallow while I concentrate on other knits. That means I often have dozens of works in progress – or WIPs – lying around that I could pick up at any time, if only I had time! I love the knitting bit but sometimes feel a bit deflated when I cast off, because I don't really want it to be finished.

But I'm not 100% process knitter either – I couldn't just knit, unravel and reknit the same piece over and over again just for the sake of it, I always have a final product in mind. The point of all this is that knitting makes us feel good. Even the most determined product knitter is knitting because it is something they want to do – and they want to do it because it feels great.

Knitting can help. Take time to knit: make a cup of tea, sit down somewhere comfortable and quiet and pick up your needles.

KNITTING IS GOOD FOR YOU

From time to time stories will hit the headlines telling us that one study or another has shown how beneficial knitting is for our health. UK-based physiotherapist and whole-body medicine advocate Betsan Corkhill has carried out some of the most comprehensive research into the health benefits of knitting through her Stitchlinks project, which she published in her book *Knit for Health and Wellness*. Stitchlinks is a non-profit community organisation that is pioneering research into the therapeutic benefits of knitting, with the aim of providing resources for clinicians, teachers and others using crafts as therapy, and also operates as a supportive community.

The project promotes ways knitting can help with pain, stress, depression, addiction and dementia. Among benefits too numerous to mention here, it cites the way it occupies the brain and hands, the soothing feeling of soft yarn passing over your skin and the space created by the arms held out in front of the body to knit.

Anecdotally, knitters tell how their craft has lifted depression, eased anxiety and helped with chronic pain. During the Covid-19 crisis and lockdowns in 2020 and 2021, newcomers and lapsed knitters took up their needles in droves all over the globe to combat anxiety and boredom, and week after week news reports flooded in saying it was the go-to hobby of the pandemic.

Life can be tough. It can be too busy or too empty. Sometimes it feels as if you are paddling against the current and getting nowhere. Sometimes it feels so filled with chaos you don't know where to turn. Knitting can help. Take time to knit: make a cup of tea, sit down somewhere comfortable and quiet and pick up your needles. Feel the rhythm of the stitches and the softness of the yarn. Watch the project grow as you work, tangible evidence that you really have achieved something today. You deserve this.

HOLDING YARN

Winding yarn around your hand can help you maintain a consistent tension and make your knitting neater, quicker and easier. There are two popular ways of holding yarn: the 'English' way, in the right hand, and the 'continental' way, in the left hand. Both mean a slightly different way of knitting. Experiment to see which you prefer.

THE ENGLISH METHOD

1 Hold both needles in your left hand. Starting with the working yarn close to the needle, wind it once around the little finger of your right hand.

2 Thread it under the ring finger and middle finger, then up and over the index finger.

3 Take the right-hand needle in your right hand and you're ready to go. As you work, you will move your hand to bring the yarn around the needle. The movement is likely to grow less and less the more experienced you become.

THE CONTINENTAL METHOD

1 Hold the needle you are about to work in your left hand. Starting with the working yarn close to the needle, wind it once around the little finger of your left hand.

2 Thread it under the ring finger and middle finger, then up and over the index finger.

3 Your right hand is free to pick up the right-hand needle and start working. Knitting in this way feels more like picking up the working yarn and pulling it through the stitch than winding it around the needle.

SLIPKNOT

To start off, you'll need to make a slipknot, as shown below. This is a flexible knot holding a loop that will act as your first stitch. If you don't put a needle into your slipknot and start knitting, you can undo it by pulling the ends – this is also a handy magic trick!

MAKE A SLIPKNOT

1 Find the end of your wool and cross the short end over the yarn attached to the ball, which is called the working yarn.

2 Now take the working yarn and push a loop of it through the loop you have just created.

3 Pull on the end of the yarn to tighten the knot holding the loop in place.

4 Slide the slipknot you have created on to your knitting needle to start casting on – or if you feel like it, pull on both ends of yarn and make the slipknot disappear, just like magic!

CASTING ON

The knitted-on cast on is useful because it uses many of the same moves as the knit stitch, so you can practise before you even start. The long-tail method creates a stretchier edge.

KNITTED-ON CAST ON

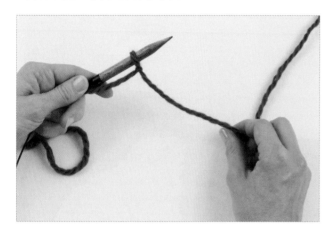

1 Start with your slipknot. Slip it on to your left-hand needle and tighten it to fit, but not so that it doesn't move easily along the needle.

2 Keeping your slipknot on the left-hand needle, insert your right-hand needle into the loop, from left to right, underneath the left-hand needle. (If it is tricky to do this, your slipknot is too tight – tug on the loop to loosen it.)

3 Bring the working yarn clockwise underneath the right-hand needle and back over the top, so you make a loop around it closer to the needle tips than the original slipknot. Use the tip of the right-hand needle to pull this new loop through the original slipknot.

4 Bring this new loop around to the tip of the left-hand needle and slip it on. You now have two stitches on the left-hand needle. To cast on more stitches, insert your right-hand needle into this new stitch and repeat steps 2–4. Repeat as many times as your pattern calls for.

TOP TIP

If you need your cast on to be stretchy, use a long-tail cast on.
If you want something firmer, try the knitted-on cast on.

LONG-TAIL CAST ON

1 To start a long-tail cast on, make a slipknot in your yarn, leaving a long tail of around 1in (2.5cm) for each stitch to be cast on, and slip it on to your needle.

2 With your left hand, create a slingshot shape by pointing your index finger and wrapping the working yarn clockwise over it, then raising your thumb and wrapping the tail anticlockwise over that. Curl the remaining three fingers in to grasp the yarn ends.

3 Use the needle tip to pick up the strand of yarn around the outside of your thumb, forming a loop.

4 Then pick up the strand of yarn on the inside of your index finger and pull it through the loop.

5 Let the yarn go and pull to tighten, but not too tight. You now have two stitches cast on. Repeat steps 2–5 until you have cast on the required number of stitches.

KNIT STITCH

The knit stitch is the basic building block of knitting. If you can work a knit stitch, you can knit: it's that simple.

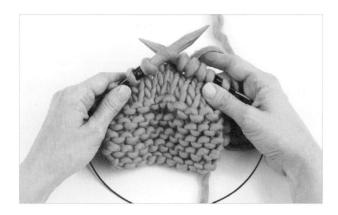

1 Hold the needle with the stitches on in your left hand and insert the tip of the right-hand needle into the first stitch, underneath the left-hand needle. The needle goes through the stitch from left to right, even though the needle itself moves from right to left.

2 Take the working yarn underneath and back over the right-hand needle in a clockwise direction, creating a loop in front of the stitch that is holding both needles.

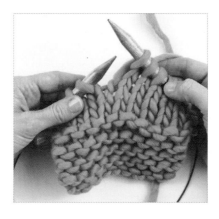

3 Now use the tip of the right-hand needle to pull this loop through the original stitch.

4 The loop on your right-hand needle is the new stitch. Slip the original stitch off the end of the left-hand needle and let it fall. It now forms part of the fabric you are knitting.

5 Repeat steps 1–4 with the next stitch on the left-hand needle and then the following one until you have knitted every stitch. To knit the next row, simply turn the work around, take the right-hand needle – now with all the stitches on – in your left hand and start all over again.

PURL STITCH

The purl stitch is the mirror image of the knit stitch. All knitting patterns, no matter how complicated, are created from the building blocks of the knit and purl stitches.

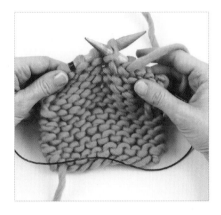

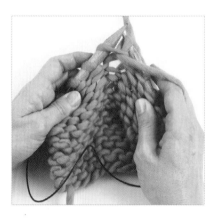

1 Insert the tip of your right-hand needle into the front of the first stitch on the left-hand needle from right to left, with the right-hand needle above the left-hand needle.

2 Take the working yarn clockwise underneath the right-hand needle tip and back over it, creating a new loop in front of the stitch being worked.

3 Pull the right-hand needle tip back out of the stitch, taking the new loop of yarn with it. This is now the new stitch.

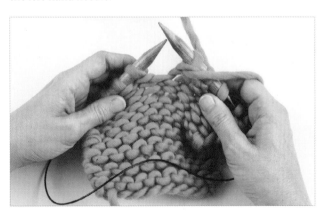

4 Let the original stitch slip off the left-hand needle to form part of the fabric.

5 Repeat steps 1–4 in the next stitch on the left-hand needle, and then the next, until all stitches have been purled. The fabric will look bobbly on the purled side and smoother on the knitted side. If you knit all the right-side rows and purl all the wrong-side rows, it is called stocking stitch, this is the most common stitch pattern you will see.

CASTING OFF

Bind off your knits securely by lifting each live stitch over the next.

1 Start by working the first two stitches as normal: if it is a knit stitch, knit it; if it is a purl stitch, purl it unless your pattern says otherwise.

2 Use the tip of your left-hand needle to lift the first stitch on the right-hand needle up and over the top of the second stitch and off the end of the right-hand needle. This stitch is now cast off.

3 Knit the next stitch on the left-hand needle so that you again have two stitches on the right-hand needle, then repeat step 2.

4 Keep repeating step 3 until you have one stitch left on the right-hand needle and none on the left-hand needle. Pass the rest of the ball, or the end of the working yarn, through this last stitch, using your fingers to make the stitch big enough for the ball to fit through, then pull tightly on the working yarn. You should have a neat and tidy row of cast-off stitches.

BLOCKING

Blocking will help turn your finished project from a scrumple into a work of fibre art.

Blocking is a hotly debated topic among knitters, and one that is shrouded in mystery. Many designers will keep their blocking methods very strictly under wraps.

Some knits just don't need it – they come off the needles beautiful and ready to wear. But others come out of casting off crumpled, skewed and generally disappointing. Blocking is what will turn these projects into the finished knit you dreamed of when you cast on. It is particularly essential for lace knits, as it opens up all the eyelets, but it is not always ideal for cables because you don't want to flatten them.

Everyone has their own method of blocking: I was taught to press finished knits under a wet tea towel with a hot iron. This is something I would never do now that I know how much love and care goes into producing the wool I knit with, let alone the knitting – that is, not unless everything else fails.

Some knitters swear by a blast from the steam iron, while others will bung a finished knit on the hand-wash cycle of their washing machine and see how it comes out. There is all manner of blocking paraphernalia you can use to get knits perfect, including specialist blocking mats, rustproof T-pins, blocking wires, specialist sprays and much more.

But if you don't want to invest in all that equipment, you don't need to. Children's interlocking playmats are a cheaper alternative to knitters' blocking mats, although they don't have the measurement grids some people swear by. I simply use my bed. In the box on the right, I've outlined my own blocking method.

METHOD
- Cover your bed in clean towels.
- Very slightly dampen your finished project – not so much that it will soak through the towels to your mattress.
- Use dressmakers' pins or T-pins to pin out the garment on top of the towels to the correct measurements.
- Spray all over with Soak Flatter or an alternative smoothing spray.
- Cover with wet tea towels or, even better, baby muslins, and leave until completely dry.

Note: this process is best started in the morning to give the knit the chance to dry before bedtime. Of course, if you have space somewhere other than your own bed, you can block at any time!

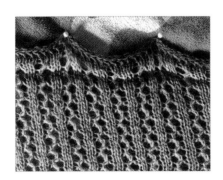

EASY DOES IT CAPELET

THERE'S REALLY NOTHING TO THIS SIMPLE CAPELET – IT'S A BRILLIANT BEGINNERS' KNIT. SIMPLY CAST ON, THEN KNIT AND KNIT UNTIL IT'S AS LONG AS YOU WANT IT TO BE. TO MAKE THIS PROJECT MORE APPROACHABLE, THIS IS DESIGNED AS A BUTTON PONCHO, SO CHOOSE BUTTONS THAT WILL FIT THROUGH THE HOLES THAT NATURALLY APPEAR IN THE KNITTING. IF YOU LIKE KNITTING IT AND WANT TO CONTINUE, JUST CARRY ON UNTIL IT'S LONG ENOUGH TO BE A WRAP OR SUPER SCARF YOU CAN WEAR WITHOUT BUTTONING – BUT YOU WILL NEED MORE YARN FOR THIS.

ABOUT THIS YARN

Erika Knight's Fat Maxi Wool is an easy, chunky knitting yarn made from hardwearing British wool that is still soft enough to wear next to the skin.

TECHNIQUES

Casting on – page 18
Knit stitch – page 20
Casting off – page 22

SIZE

Width: 44½in (113cm)
Depth: 15¾in (40cm)
Before blocking: 15in (38cm) deep, 44¾in (114cm) wide

TENSION

9 sts and 18 rows to 4in (10cm) over garter stitch (knit every row).
Tension is not critical to this project.

YOU WILL NEED

Erika Knight Fat Maxi Wool
100% pure British wool
(approx 87yd/80m per 100g)
6 x 100g skeins in 219 Mulberry
10mm (UK000:US15) needles
6 x ½in (12mm) diameter buttons
(to fit through ordinary stitches)
Yarn needle
3 x ¾in (20mm) diameter buttons
Sewing needle and matching thread

Note: Yarn amounts are based on average requirements and are approximate.

ABBREVIATIONS

See page 148.

PONCHO

Cast on 36 sts.
Row 1 (RS): Knit.
Row 2 (WS): Knit.
Cont as set, knitting every row until piece meas 44½in (113cm).
Cast off.

TO FINISH

Weave in loose ends (see page 71). Sew 3 buttons the right size to fit through ordinary holes between stitches along cast-on or cast-off edge. Wear buttoned or unbuttoned.

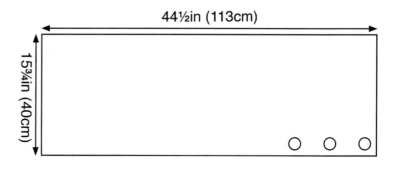

KNITTING IN THE ROUND

There are a few ways to knit in the round: you can use several double-pointed needles or a circular needle exactly the right size for your knit. The magic loop method is handy because you can use the same circular needle for any size of knitting.

1 Cast on the number of stitches you want and slide them on to the connecting cable of your circular needle.

2 Find the middle of the stitches and pull the cable out through this point, but not so far that any stitches drop off the ends of the needle tips.

3 Leave the half of the stitches connected to the working yarn on the cable – these will be known as the back stitches. Slide the other half of the stitches onto the left-hand needle tip. These are the front stitches.

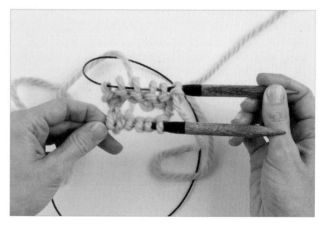

4 Bring the right-hand needle tip around and knit the first stitch on the left-hand needle tip. Pull the working yarn tightly afterwards; you will find your stitches have joined in a loop. It is a good idea to place a marker at this point so that you know where your round begins and ends.

5 Carry on knitting until you have worked all the front stitches. Taking care not to turn the stitches you have worked upside down or inside out, turn the work around so that the stitches you have just knitted are now sitting at the back on the left-hand needle tip and the cast-on stitches are at the front on the cable.

JOGLESS JOIN

Sometimes, joining in the round can leave a gap or irregularity that needs to be patched up at the end of the project. This simple trick is a way to avoid that and create a really neat join.

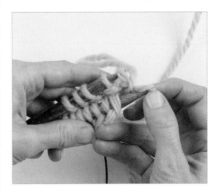

6 Pull the cable until the cast-on stitches now at the front of the work are sitting on the needle tip in front of the other needle tip. This is now your left-hand needle. Take care not to drop any stitches at this point. Pull the needle tip at the back out of the back stitches so that they now sit on the cable. This is now your right-hand needle tip. Bring this needle tip around and work the first stitch on the left-hand needle. Carry on knitting until you have worked all the stitches on the needle tip. You have now knitted one round. Repeat for as many rounds as you like, creating a neat tube of knitting.

1 Cast on one more stitch than you need. Once the stitches have been distributed across your needles, slip the last cast-on stitch on to the first needle.

2 Use your fingers or a needle tip to pass the first cast-on stitch over the last cast-on stitch.

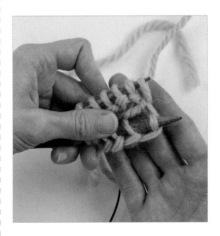

3 Now return the last cast-on stitch to its original needle. The result is a really neat, tight join.

TOP TIP
When knitting in the round, avoid ladders of loose stitches by making sure you move the gap between needles regularly. A simple way to do this is to slide the cable out so that all the stitches line up, then pull it out at a different point to continue your magic loop.

BEGINNER'S COWL

THIS CUTE AND COSY COWL IS A GREAT INTRODUCTION TO KNITTING IN THE ROUND. IT KNITS UP QUICKLY AND EASILY, IN A SUPER-SOFT, SUPER-CHUNKY MERINO WOOL, GIVING YOU A GREAT SENSE OF QUICK ACHIEVEMENT. AND IT MAKES A WONDERFUL GIFT.

ABOUT THIS YARN

Malabrigo is a family-owned company based in Uruguay and Peru, making beautifully soft and vibrant hand-dyed yarns that sell all over the world. The company employs mainly women, and tries to give jobs to people who have fewer opportunities than most.

YOU WILL NEED

Malabrigo Rasta 100% kettle-dyed Merino wool (approx 90yd/82m per 150g)
1 x 150g hank in 093 Fucsia
12mm (US17) circular or double-pointed needles
Stitch marker

Note: Yarn amounts given are based on average requirements and are approximate.

ABBREVIATIONS

See page 148.

NECK WARMER

Cast on 46 sts. Join to work in the round, taking care not to twist stitches, and pm to mark beg of rnd.
*Rnds 1 and 2: Purl.
Next rnd: Knit.
Rep last rnd until piece meas approx 5½in (14cm).
Purl 2 rnds.
Cast off loosely pwise.

TO FINISH

Weave in ends (see page 71).

TECHNIQUES

Casting on – page 18
Jogless join – page 27
Purl stitch – page 21
Knitting in the round – page 26
Casting off – page 22

SIZE

Circumference: 21in (53cm)
Depth: 6¾in (17cm)

TENSION

9 sts and 12 rnds to 4 in (10cm) over st st.
Use larger or smaller needles if necessary to obtain correct tension.

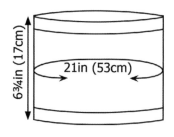

INCREASING

'Make one left' (m1L) creates a left-slanted increase, whereas 'make one right' (m1R) creates a right-slanted increase. If you work a 'knit front and back' (kfb) increase at the end of each row your fabric will become wider. Working increases and decreases one stitch in from the edge gives you a smooth, neat edge to your work.

MAKE ONE LEFT (M1L)

1 Knit the first stitch on the needle, then look for the bar that sits between this stitch and the next on the left-hand needle. Insert the tip of the right-hand needle from front to back through this bar, pick it up and slip it on to the tip of the left-hand needle.

2 Knit this new stitch through the back loop (see facing page). This twists it and avoids a hole.

MAKE ONE RIGHT (M1R)

1 Knit to the last stitch on the left-hand needle, then look for the bar between this stitch and the last stitch on the right-hand needle. Insert the tip of the right-hand needle from back to front into this bar, pick it up and slip it on to the tip of the left-hand needle.

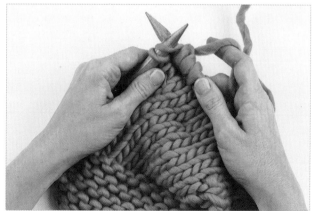

2 Knit this stitch through the front loop. This twists it and avoids a hole.

KNIT FRONT AND BACK (KFB)

1 Before you begin, take a look at the first stitch on your left-hand needle. The front of the loop (on the side of the needle facing you) should be a little in front of the back of the loop. These are also known as the front and back legs of the stitch. Start off by knitting the first stitch through its front loop as normal, but do not slip the stitch off the end of the left-hand needle.

2 Keeping the original stitch on the left-hand needle and the new stitch on the right-hand needle, take the right-hand needle tip to the back of the left-hand needle and inscrt it into the back loop of the original stitch.

3 Wrap the yarn around and pull the new loop through as you would in the knit stitch, then slip the original stitch off the end of the left-hand needle. You now have two stitches on the right-hand needle knitted from just one stitch on the left-hand needle. If you work this increase at each end of the row, your fabric will get wider.

KTBL

Knitting through the back loop can close a gap or twist a stitch to make it stand out.

Most of the time when you knit you insert the tip of the right-hand needle into the front loop of the stitch you are knitting. Inserting the needle tip into the back of the stitch, as shown here, is called 'knitting through the back loop' and twists the stitch, which can give it extra definition. Sometimes this technique is used to untwist stitches that have ended up twisted for one reason or another.

DECREASING

'Knit two together' (k2tog) is the simplest decrease and creates a right-leaning stitch. You can purl two together in a similar way. 'Slip, slip, knit' (ssk) makes a left-leaning decrease. 'Slip one, knit two together, pass slipped stitch over' (sk2po) makes a double decrease.

KNIT TWO TOGETHER (K2TOG)

1 Instead of inserting your needle into just one stitch, insert it into the next two stitches on the left-hand needle, just as if you were going to knit a single stitch. Wrap the working yarn around the needle and pull the new loop through the original two stitches.

2 Slip them off the end of the left-hand needle, just as you would if you were knitting a single stitch. You have now made two stitches into one stitch.

SLIP, SLIP, KNIT (SSK)

1 Insert the tip of the right-hand needle into the next stitch on the left-hand needle as if to knit it, but instead just slip it from the left-hand needle to the right-hand needle.

2 Repeat with the next stitch so you have two slipped stitches on the right-hand needle. Insert the left-hand needle through both those stitches from left to right on top of the right-hand needle. Wrap the working yarn around the right-hand needle, knitting the two slipped stitches together through the back loop, and slip them off the end of the left-hand needle.

SLIP ONE, KNIT TWO TOGETHER, PASS SLIPPED STITCH OVER (SK2PO)

  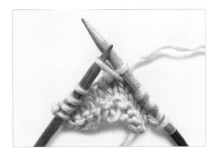

1 Slip the next stitch from the left to the right-hand needle as if to knit.

2 Knit the following two stitches together.

3 Pass the slipped stitch over.

TASSELS

Adorn any knit with these simple yet effective decorations.

1 Decide how many tassels you want. Cut double the amount of pieces of yarn – 14in (36cm) is a good length. Split the yarns into pairs and fold them in half to give you four-stranded tassels. Use pins to mark the points where you want each tassel. Take a tassel and use your fingers to push the folded part of it, from front to back, through one of the edge stitches of the shawl. This creates a loop on the wrong side.

2 Thread the cut ends through this loop, then pull tight. Trim the ends to tidy them up.

3 The result is a lovely neat tassel.

MOUNTAIN SHAWL

SOMETIMES, LEARNING A NEW TECHNIQUE CAN FEEL LIKE CLIMBING A MOUNTAIN – AND ONCE YOU'VE LEARNED IT YOU CAN FEEL THAT SAME HEADY FEELING OF ACHIEVEMENT. THIS SIMPLE, CHUNKY SHAWL INTRODUCES INCREASES AND DECREASES AND IS KNITTED SIDEWAYS TO CREATE A WIDE TRIANGLE SHAPE, FINISHED OFF WITH TRENDY TASSELS.

ABOUT THIS YARN

Wool and the Gang started life in London with a mission to inspire the next generation of makers by changing the craft experience and making it more welcoming. Its super chunky Crazy Sexy Wool is made from 100% super-soft South American fleeces.

TECHNIQUES

Slipknot – page 17
Knitting through the back loop – page 31
Knit stitch – page 20
Purl stitch – page 21
Increasing – page 30
Decreasing – page 32
Tassels – page 33

SIZE

Width: 96in (244cm)
Depth: 23in (58cm)

TENSION

7 sts x 14 rows to 4in (10cm) over g st.
Tension is not critical to this project.

YOU WILL NEED

Wool and the Gang Crazy Sexy Wool
100% wool (approx 87yd/80m per 200g)
4 x 200g balls in Pink Sherbet
12mm (US17) needles
Stitch markers

Note: Yarn amounts are based on average requirements and are approximate.

ABBREVIATIONS

See page 148.

SHAWL

Make a slipknot and place it on the LH needle (1 st).
Row 1: Knit into the front, back and front of the stitch to increase 2 (3 sts).
Row 2: Purl.
Row 3: K2, m1R, k1 (4 sts).
Row 4: Purl.
Row 5: K2, m1R, k2 (5 sts).
Row 6: P2, k1, p2.
Row 7: Knit.
Row 8: As row 6.

SET INCREASE PATTERN

Row 1 (RS): K to last 2 sts, m1R, k2 (inc 1).
Rows 2 and 4: P2, k to last 2 sts, p2.
Row 3: Knit.
Rep these 4 rows until you have 38 sts, ending with row 4. Piece meas approx 48in (122cm).

SET DECREASE PATTERN

Row 1 (RS): K to last 4 sts, k2tog, k2 (dec 1).
Rows 2 and 4: P2, k to last 2 sts, p2.
Row 3: Knit.
Rep these 4 rows until 5 sts rem, ending with row 4.
Next row (RS): K2, k2tog, k1 (4 sts).
Next row: Purl.
Next row: K1, k2tog, k1 (3 sts).
Next row: Purl.
Next row: K3tog.
Fasten off.

TO FINISH

Weave in ends (see page 71).
Block to desired measurements (see page 23).
Make tassels, attach to hem.

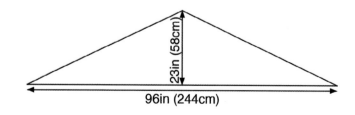

CABLES

Cables use an extra needle with two pointed ends called a cable needle to move stitches from one place to another. There are two basic types – with the cable needle held at the back or the front of the work – but endless variations.

CABLE FOUR FRONT (C4F)

1 Slip the next two stitches to a cable needle held at the front of the work.

2 Leaving these two stitches, knit the following two stitches as normal.

3 Now knit the two stitches on the cable needle.

4 You have created a left-leaning cable.

CABLE FOUR BACK (C4B)

1 Slip the next two stitches to a cable needle held at the back of the work.

2 Leaving these two stitches, knit the following two stitches as normal.

3 Now knit the two stitches on the cable needle.

4 You have created a right-leaning cable.

TOP TIP
Always follow the instructions carefully, and make sure you read abbreviations with care because there are all sorts of ways of expressing all the different cables there are.

TWISTS

In knitting, 'twists' can refer to all sorts of different things, but in this book the name is used for two-stitch cables that don't use a cable needle. They can be a little fiddly to work, but the technique saves all that time you spend looking for your cable needle when it goes missing.

TWISTING STITCHES

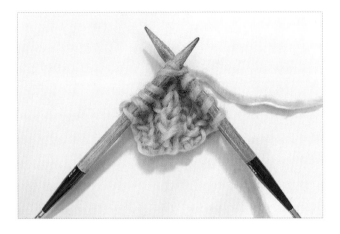

1 Take the yarn to the back of the work and insert the right-hand needle tip into the second stitch on the left-hand needle. Knit the stitch but do not slip it off the needle.

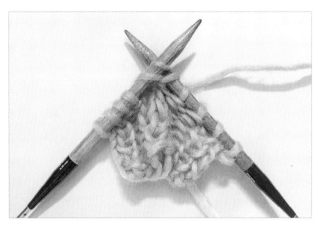

2 Now insert the right-hand needle tip into the first stitch on the left-hand needle and knit it.

3 Slip both knitted stitches off the left-hand needle at the same time.

4 The result is a pair of stitches that cross over each other to create a little twist in the fabric.

YARN OVERS

Yarn overs form the basis of all lace knitting. They can be used to create decorative eyelets or as an alternative way of increasing. They work slightly differently depending on the stitch that follows and they sometimes have different names but in this book they are all called yarn overs.

YARN OVER BEFORE A KNIT STITCH

Also known as yarn forward (yf or yfwd), yarn over needle (yon).

1 After your last stitch bring the yarn to the front of the work...

2 ...then knit the next stitch as normal, taking the working yarn over the top of the needle to the back of the work.

3 The working yarn has created a new stitch, which you can work as if it were a normal stitch on the next row.

4 This leaves a little hole in the fabric. It works in exactly the same way if you are working a knit decrease in your next stitch, even if you are slipping a stitch before you work your knit decrease. To avoid a hole, you can work the yarn over through the back loop on the next row.

TOP TIP
Yarn overs are easy to do but it can be alarming to work into such a loose stitch and to leave holes in your knitting. Just keep your cool and it will all work out fine!

YARN OVER BEFORE A PURL STITCH

Also known as yarn round needle (yrn), yarn over and round needle (yorn).

1 After your last stitch bring the yarn to the front of the needle if it isn't there already.

2 Take it over the needle to the back of the work, then bring it between the needles to the front of the work.

3 Purl the next stitch as normal.

4 On the next row, work the yarn over as if it were a normal stitch to create an eyelet, or work it through the back loop to avoid a hole. The yarn over works in the same way if you are working a purl decrease on the following stitch.

COSY RUANA

THIS GARMENT IS A CROSS BETWEEN A SHAWL, A CARDIGAN AND A BLANKET – THE PERFECT WAY TO BLEND STYLE AND COSINESS. IT'S A SIMPLE KNIT THAT WILL GIVE YOU LOTS OF TIME TO ENJOY THE GORGEOUSLY SOFT WOOL, AND AS IT'S FAIRLY CHUNKY IT WILL KNIT UP IN A RELATIVELY SHORT TIME TOO. IT'S A GREAT WAY TO LEARN SOME SIMPLE TWISTS AND BUILD UP YOUR CONFIDENCE FOR MORE CHALLENGING CABLE PROJECTS.

ABOUT THIS YARN
We Are Knitters is the brainchild of Spanish friends Alberto Bravo and Pepita Marín, who spotted a young girl knitting on the New York subway – and came up with a bold business idea to spread the word about the craft. The Petite Wool is super-soft and made from 100% wool.

YOU WILL NEED
We Are Knitters The Petite Wool
100% wool (approx 153yd/140m per 100g)
10 x 100g balls in Sprinkle Denim
8mm (UK0:US1) needles

Note: Yarn amounts given are based on average requirements and are approximate.

ABBREVIATIONS
See page 148.

SPECIAL ABBREVIATION
TW2 = knit into the second st on the LH needle with the RH needle in front of the first st, do not slip st off the needle, k into first st on LH needle, slip both sts off needle together.

TECHNIQUES
Casting on – page 18
Knit stitch – page 20
Purl stitch – page 21
Twists – page 37
Cables – page 36
Casting off – page 22

SIZE
Width: 47¼in (120cm)
Depth: 61½in (156cm)

TENSION
11.5 sts and 16 rows to 4in (10cm) over st st. *Use larger or smaller needles if necessary to obtain correct tension.*

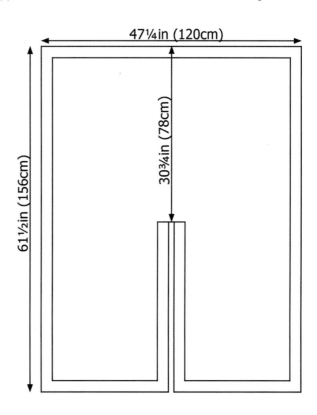

47¼in (120cm)

30¾in (78cm)

61½in (156cm)

RUANA

Cast on 146 sts.

SET RIB PATT

Row 1 (RS): (K2, p2) to last 2 sts, k2.

Row 2: (P2, k2) to last 2 sts, p2.

Row 3: (K2, p2, TW2, p2) to last 2 sts, k2.

Row 4: As row 2.

Rep rows 1–4 once more.

Piece meas approx 2¼in (6cm).

SET MAIN PATT

Row 1 (RS): (K2, p2) twice, k to last 8 sts, (p2, k2) twice.

Row 2: (P2, k2) twice, p to last 8 sts, (k2, p2) twice.

Row 3: K2, p2, TW2, p2, k to last 8 sts, p2, TW2, p2, k2.

Row 4: As row 2.

Rep rows 1–4 until piece meas approx 30¾in (78cm), ending with row 4.

SET UP FRONT SPLIT

Row 1 (RS): (K2, p2), twice, k57, p2, k2, p2, k4, p2, k2, p2, k to last 8 sts, (p2, k2) twice.

Row 2: (P2, k2) twice, p57, k2, p2, k2, p4, k2, p2, k2, p to last 8 sts, (k2, p2) twice.

Next row (RS): K2, p2, TW2, p2, k57, p2, TW2, p2, k2, slip rem sts to a holder or scrap yarn, turn and work on first 73 sts only for right front.

RIGHT FRONT

Next row (WS): (P2, k2) twice, p to last 8 sts, (k2, p2) twice.

Next row (RS): K2, p2, TW2, p2, k to last 9 sts, kfb, p2, TW2, p2, k2 (74 sts).

**Next row: As row 2 of main patt. Cont in main patt as set by rows 1–4 above until piece meas approx 59in (150cm).

Work rib patt as set above, rep rows 1–4 twice.

Cast off in rib.

LEFT FRONT

With WS facing, slip rem 73 sts back to needles and rejoin yarn.

Next row (WS): (P2, k2) twice, p to last 8 sts, (k2, p2) twice.

Next row (RS): K2, p2, TW2, p2, kfb, k to last 8 sts, p2, TW2, p2, k2 (74 sts).

Work as for right front from ** to end.

TO FINISH

Weave in ends (see page 71).

Block (see page 23).

BEDTIME WRAP

THIS COSY WRAP IN A LIGHT AND AIRY, SUPER-SOFT BRITISH WOOL DOUBLES AS A BED RUNNER OR SNUGGLE BLANKET, AND INTRODUCES SOME SIMPLE BUT BEAUTIFULLY EFFECTIVE CABLES. TO MAKE IT EVEN MORE RELAXING, YOU COULD PLACE STITCH MARKERS (SEE PAGE 47) ON EITHER SIDE OF THE CABLE PANELS SO YOU DON'T HAVE TO COUNT WHEN YOU'RE WORKING THE SIMPLE REVERSE STOCKING STITCH SECTION BETWEEN THEM.

ABOUT THIS YARN

West Yorkshire Spinners makes yarns from British wools, and its super-soft roving Re:Treat is designed to be comforting and relaxing to knit with – an instant wellness boost.

TECHNIQUES

Casting on – page 18
Knit stitch – page 20
Purl stitch – page 21
Cables – page 36
Casting off – page 22

SIZE

Width: 71in (180cm)
Depth: 23½in (60cm)

TENSION

12 sts and 16 rows to 4in (10cm) over rev st st. *Tension is not critical to this project.*

YOU WILL NEED

West Yorkshire Spinners Re:Treat
100% British wool
(approx 157yd/140m per 100g)
6 x 100g balls in Ponder
6.5mm (UK3:US10½) needles
Cable needle

Note: Yarn amounts are based on average requirements and are approximate.

ABBREVIATIONS

See page 148.

SPECIAL ABBREVIATIONS

C3B = cable 3 back: slip next 2 sts to cn and hold at back of work, k1, k2 from cn
C3F = cable 3 front: slip next 1 st to cn and hold at front of work, k2, k1 from cn
C4B = cable 4 back: slip next 2 sts to cn and hold at back of work, k2, k2 from cn
C4F = cable 4 front: slip next 2 sts to cn and hold at front of work, k2, k2 from cn

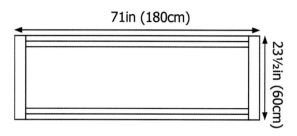

71in (180cm) · 23½in (60cm)

CABLE PANEL

| | 18 | 17 | 16 | 15 | 14 | 13 | 12 | 11 | 10 | 9 | 8 | 7 | 6 | 5 | 4 | 3 | 2 | 1 | |

KEY

☐ RS: knit, WS: purl
• RS: purl, WS: knit
⤸ C3B
⤵ C3F
⤸ C4B
⤵ C4F

CABLE PANEL

Worked over 18 sts and 4 rows

Row 1: C3B, p3, C4B, k2, p3, C3F.

Row 2 and all alt rows: P3, k3, p6, k3, p3.

Row 3: K3, p3, k2, C4F, p3, k3.

WRAP

Cast on 88 sts.

SET RIB

Rib row 1: (K2, p2) 3 times, p1, k3, p3, k2, p2, k2, p3, k3, (p2, k2) 6 times, p2, k3, p3, k2, p2, k2, p3, k3, p1, (p2, k2) 3 times.

Rib row 2: (P2, k2) 3 times, k1, p3, k3, p2, k2, p2, k3, p3, k2, (p2, k2) 6 times, p3, k3, p2, k2, p2, k3, p3, k1, (k2, p2) 3 times.

These 2 rows set rib.

Rep these 2 rows until piece meas approx 2½in (6cm), ending with row 2.

***Next row (RS):** (K2, p2) 3 times, p1, k3, p3, k6, p3, k3, p26, k3, p3, k6, p3, k3, p1, (p2, k2) 3 times.

Next row: (P2, k2) 3 times, k1, p3, k3, p6, k3, p3, k26, p3, k3, p6, k3, p3, k1, (k2, p2) 3 times.*

SET CABLE PATTERN

Row 1 (RS): (K2, p2) 3 times, p1, work Cable Panel row 1 over next 18 sts, p26, work Cable Panel row 1 over next 18 sts, p1, (p2, k2) 3 times.

Row 2: (P2, k2) 3 times, k1, work Cable Panel row 2 over next 18 sts, k26, work Cable Panel row 2 over next 18 sts, k1, (k2, p2) 3 times.

Row 3: (K2, p2) 3 times, p1, work Cable Panel row 3 over next 18 sts, p26, work Cable Panel row 3 over next 18 sts, p1, (p2, k2) 3 times.

Row 4: (P2, k2) 3 times, k1, work Cable Panel row 4 over next 18 sts, k26, work Cable Panel row 4 over next 18 sts, k1, (k2, p2) 3 times.

These 4 rows set patt. Cont in patt as set until piece meas approx 68in (173cm), ending with row 2.

SET END BORDER

Rep from * to * once.

Rep 2 rib rows to match rib border at cast-on edge. Piece should meas approx 71in (180cm).

Cast off in rib.

TO FINISH

Weave in ends (see page 71).

Block gently (see page 23).

STITCH MARKERS

Keep track of your knitting with a collection of bright jewels.

Stitch markers can be anything from a little loop of scrap yarn or a safety pin to a pretty earring or a specially designed ring. Lots of companies produce them, but you can also find quirky, sustainably produced and imaginative handmade versions on makers' platforms such as Etsy and at yarn fairs and festivals.

The designs in this book suggest that you place markers at points where increases or decreases need to be worked, or where simple stocking stitch or garter stitch sections give way to panels of more complicated stitches, so you don't need to count every stitch but can just relax and drift away as you work.

The photograph below shows a classic triangle shawl, with stitch markers placed at the edge of each border and on each side of the central spine – that is, at every point where a yarn over needs to be made on every right-side row, and where you switch from knit to purl on every wrong side row, to create garter stitch and stocking stitch sections.

All the stitch markers in this picture are designed to mark a point in the knitting as it goes along, so they sit on the needles and pass from one needle tip to the other. Sometimes, opening stitch markers, like tiny safety pins, are used to mark a point in the knitted fabric. In this case, they are opened, inserted into the stitch to be marked, and closed.

Sometimes stitch markers aren't mentioned in some pattern rows – in that case, just slip them from one needle to another and carry on until they are mentioned again.

MIND OVER **KNITTER**

Your yarn and needles could be the gateway to a healing meditation practice.

The buzzwords meditation and mindfulness are becoming ever more popular. As stress levels rise and more and more people suffer with anxiety and depression, clinicians, therapists and practitioners are recommending mindfulness practice and meditation to more and more people.

But for some people meditation is a real struggle. Maybe it opens up troubling feelings they are not ready to deal with, or they simply can't sit still or quieten their minds enough to focus. That is where knitting can help. It can provide a focus you can keep coming

back to every time your mind drifts, and a reminder of what you are doing when your busy brain wants to rush off somewhere else at a rate of knots.

THE HEALING POWERS

Food writer and broadcaster turned knitwear designer and yarn dyer James McIntosh was struck down and left housebound by depression. While stuck at home he discovered knitting, and the joy of learning and making helped him to recover. Since then he has published a book of knitwear designs and recipes called

Knit and Nibble, created his own yarn brand, McIntosh Yarn, and travels all over the world to promote his practice of Knititation.

Knititation focuses on the mindful presence James was able to find in knitting. He struggles to follow standard meditations because his brain tends to be too quick and busy – but with his needles in hand he is able to anchor himself in the present moment, focusing on the feeling of the yarn, the sensation of his bottom on a seat and the rhythm of the stitches he is making.

In the US, New York-based Heart Knit goes into corporate businesses, teaching simple knitting, stretching and breathing exercises to help stressed workers relax through the power of knitting. Yoga teacher and crafter Suzan Colón teaches MedKNITation to packed classes at yarn festivals and sells audio meditations online. These have been so popular that at the first ever Virtual Knitting Live event run by *Vogue Knitting* magazine during the Covid-19 pandemic lockdown, Suzan led daily free meditation sessions for event-goers.

STITCHES AND MANTRAS

Suzan's practice focuses on the knitting itself, encouraging crafters to bring the rhythm of their breathing in line with the rhythm of their stitches and to focus fully on the formation of each individual stitch or repeated stitch pattern. She also suggests repeating a mantra as you knit, bringing a positive message into the meditation.

Incorporating regular stretches into your knitting habits is another way of changing the focus of a busy brain, being kind to your body and encouraging mindfulness of the present moment. Wrist, arm and shoulder stretches and gentle rotations are important, but it's also great to stand up once in a while, reach for the sky and take a full body stretch to loosen up aching muscles and get the blood flowing.

Whether you're an experienced meditator, a complete newbie or someone who has tried and failed to engage in this healing practice before, it is definitely worth giving knitting meditations a try.

MEET YOUR **INNER STITCHER**

Try this simple knitting meditation:

- First make sure you are sitting comfortably, in a quiet place, ideally with your back straight and both feet flat on the floor. You may want to stretch your legs, arms, shoulders and wrists gently before taking your seat. As you get settled, notice the sensations around you, ticking off all five senses as you tune into yourself, as well as how you are doing mentally and emotionally.

- Before picking up your knitting, take a few long, slow breaths, feeling your belly growing as the air goes in and letting it deflate completely as you let all the air out. Notice how you feel as you do this.

- Now pick up your knitting and focus fully on your stitches. Count as you work, either counting to five, then starting again from one if you are on a plain pattern, or talking through a simple repeat such as 'yarn forward, slip one, yarn over, brioche knit one'. Try to let your breathing fall into the same rhythm as your counting and stitches.

- Try to keep concentrating on your work. Distractions will come either from outside or from inside you in the form of thoughts and feelings. As they come, notice them, accept them, take note of the way they make you feel, and then let them go and return your focus to your needles. If you lose count, don't worry, just start again from one.

- You may only be able to keep this up for a minute or two at first, but as you practise you will be able to meditate for longer. Do it for as long as it feels good, then stop.

- Lay your knitting down and once again tune into all the sensations in your body. Note how you are feeling physically and emotionally, and whether this is different from the way you were feeling before your meditation. Take a few more deep breaths. Stay in this position, noticing the sensations in your body and mind, for as long as you enjoy it, then stand up, do a few quick, gentle stretches, and carry on with your day.

GARTER TAB CAST ON

A garter stitch tab is a classic way to begin a shawl. A narrow tab is made, then stitches are picked up along the side and the cast-on end to create a neat band across the top of the work that can go from edge to edge uninterrupted.

1 Cast on three stitches and knit five rows, or as many as stated in your pattern. Note that there are three purl bumps along the side of the knitted tab.

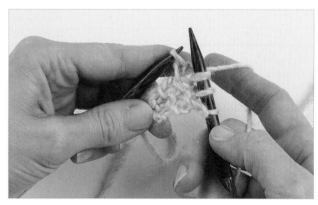

2 Without turning the work, rotate the tab 90 degrees clockwise so the side edge is facing up. Insert your right-hand needle tip into the first purl bump and pick up a stitch. If this is tricky, it may be easier to pick up the purl bump with your left-hand needle and knit it as normal.

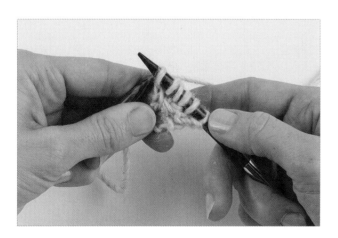

3 Repeat with the next two purl bumps. You should now have six stitches on your right-hand needle.

4 Turn the work 90 degrees clockwise again and pick up and knit three stitches along the cast-on edge. You now have nine stitches on your right-hand needle.

PICOT CAST OFF

This decorative cast off takes a while but is well worth it as it gives a very striking effect. You can use picots right across a cast off, or use single picots to accentuate certain points on your shawl edge. This method uses the cable cast on, which is explained here.

1 Start with the right side facing you and prepare to work a cable cast on by inserting your right-hand needle tip in between the first two stitches on the left-hand needle.

2 Wrap the yarn around, pull it through and slip the stitch on to the left-hand needle, casting on one stitch.

3 Repeat steps 1 and 2 to cast on a second stitch.

4 Now cast off four stitches as normal by knitting two stitches and passing the first stitch over the second, then slip the last stitch on the right-hand needle back to the left-hand needle.

5 Repeat these five steps until only one stitch remains, then fasten off. You are left with a really pretty decorative edge, which you can accentuate by pinning out the picots when blocking.

IN-FLIGHT SHAWL

THIS SINGLE-SKEIN PROJECT IS THE PERFECT KNIT TO KEEP YOUR HANDS BUSY AS YOU WATCH THE IN-FLIGHT MOVIE OR GAZE AT THE SCENERY WHILE CRUISING AT 30,000 FEET. THAT ALSO MEANS IT'S A PERFECT ANXIETY-EASER FOR NERVOUS FLIERS. SOFT AND WARM THANKS TO ITS 90% ALPACA FIBRE CONTENT, IT ALSO FEELS STRONG AND STURDY, AND WILL SCRUNCH UP TO NOTHING IN YOUR KNITTING BAG – AND IN YOUR HAND LUGGAGE ONCE IT'S FINISHED.

ABOUT THIS YARN
Devon's John Arbon is a family-run mill spinning yarns from British fleeces. Its Alpaca 2-3 Ply is soft, strong and very, very long – so you can create a beautifully cosy, lightweight shawl from just one hank of yarn.

TECHNIQUES
Garter tab cast on – page 50
Stitch markers – page 47
Knit stitch – page 20
Yarn overs – page 38
Decreasing – page 32
Picot cast off – page 51

SIZE
Width: 67in (170cm)
Depth at longest point: 29½in (75cm)

TENSION
18 sts and 44 rows to 4in (10cm) over g st and eyelet pattern. *Tension is not critical to this project.*

YOU WILL NEED
John Arbon Alpaca 2–3 Ply
90% alpaca, 10% nylon
(approx 656yd/600m per 100g)
1 x 100g skein in Merlot
4mm (UK8:US6) circular needle, 47in (120cm) long
Stitch markers

Note: Yarn amounts are based on average requirements and are approximate.

TENSION NOTE
Tension is not critical to this project. In this design, a lace-weight yarn is knitted on 4mm needles, which can feel very loose and even slightly uncomfortable. However, using larger needles gives the shawl its light, airy quality. If you are substituting yarns, try swatching on a number of different needle sizes to see what kind of fabric you are happiest with – or just cast on and see what you get! This design would also work well as a stashbuster to use up leftover lightweight yarn.

ABBREVIATIONS
See page 148.

SHAWL
Cast on 3 sts.
Knit 5 rows.
At the end of the last row rotate piece 90 degrees, pick up 3 sts along side

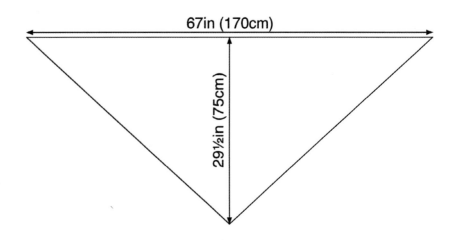

67in (170cm)

29½in (75cm)

edge, rotate 90 degrees again and pick up 3 sts along cast-on edge (9 sts).

Set-up row: K3, pm, k3, pm, k3.

SET MAIN PATTERN

Row 1 (RS): K2, yo, k to m, yo, sm, k3, sm, yo, k to last 2 sts, yo, k2 (inc 4).

Row 2: Knit.

Rep rows 1 and 2 nineteen more times (89 sts).

**SET EYELET PATTERN

Row 1: K2, yo, k1, (yo, k2tog) to m, yo, sm, k3, sm, (yo, k2tog) to last 3 sts, yo, k1, yo, k2 (inc 4).

Row 2: Knit.

Rep rows 1 and 2 of main patt 20 more times (inc 80).

Rep from ** 3 more times, then work eyelet pattern once more (425 sts).

Rep rows 1 and 2 of main patt twice more (433 sts).

PICOT CAST OFF

With RS facing, cast off as foll:
*Cast on 2 sts using the cable cast on inserting the needle tip between 2 sts on the LH needle, cast off 4 sts, then slip last st from the RH back to the LH needle; rep from * to end, then fasten off.

TO FINISH

Weave in ends (see page 71).
Block to open out eyelets
(see page 23).

SUNSHINE SHAWLETTE

THIS PURE CASHMERE OMBRÉ SHAWLETTE IS A WONDERFUL TREAT TO KNIT, MADE UP OF FIVE SPECIALLY DYED SHADES OF YELLOW. ALTHOUGH THE INCREASES LOOK ASYMMETRIC AND ESOTERIC THEY ARE EASY TO KEEP TRACK OF WITH STITCH MARKERS, MAKING THIS A TRULY RELAXING KNIT.

ABOUT THIS YARN

Abby Parkes set up Orchidean Luxury Yarns because she believes life is too short to knit with cheap yarn. She started by importing sustainably sourced cashmere produced in Italy before discovering a love of hand dyeing. Her Decadence yarn would work well for this design too.

TECHNIQUES

Garter tab cast on – page 50
Knit stitch – page 20
Stitch markers – page 47
Purl stitch – page 21
Yarn overs – page 38
Decreasing – page 32
Casting off – page 22

SIZE

Width: approx 47¼in (120cm)
Depth: 15¾in (40cm)

TENSION

22 sts and 28 rows to 4in (10cm) over st st. *Tension is not critical to this project.*

YOU WILL NEED

Orchidean Luxury Yarns Di Lusso HD Mustard Shfade set of 5 x 25g mini-skeins, 100% cashmere (approx 93yd/85m per 25g). Start with darkest shade (A) and work through the set to the lightest (E)
4mm (UK8:US6) needles
Stitch markers

Note: Yarn amounts are based on average requirements and are approximate.

ABBREVIATIONS

See page 148.

MAIN PATTERN

Row 1: (K to m, sm, yo) to last m, k to last 3 sts, yo, k3.
Row 2: K3, p to last 3 sts, k3.

SHAWL

Using A, cast on 3 sts.
Knit 12 rows.
Turn work 90 degrees, pick up and k6 sts, one in each garter bump, turn 90 degrees again, pick up 3 sts along cast-on edge (12 sts).

SET MAIN PATTERN

Set-up row 1 (WS): K3, (p2, pm) 3 times, k3.
Now work rows 1 and 2 of Main Patt until you have 56 sts, ending with a RS row 1.

TOP TIP

Work garter stitch edge stitches loosely.

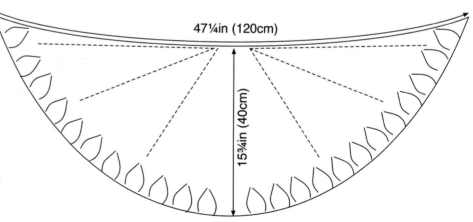

47¼in (120cm)

15¾in (40cm)

Set-up row 2 (WS): K3, p11, pm, p2, pm, p to last 3 sts slipping markers, k3. Cont in Main Patt as now set until you have 134 sts, ending with a RS row 1.

Set-up row 3 (WS): K3, p17, pm, p2, pm, p to last 3 sts slipping markers, k3. Cont in Main Patt as now set until you have 150 sts, ending on a WS row 2. Break A, join B.

Work Main Patt row 1.

Set-up row 4 (WS): K3, *p to 2 sts before m, pm, p2, sm; rep from * to last m, p to last 3 sts, k3.

Cont in Main Patt as now set, changing to C when you run out of B and changing to D when you run out of C (this can be done at the start of any row), until you have 398 sts,

ending with a RS row 1 on which you remove all markers.

SET CHEVRON PATTERN

Set-up row (WS): K3, p4, pm, p to last 7 sts, pm, p4, k3.

Row 1 (RS): K3, yo, k1, yo, k to m, sm, (k1, yo, k4, sk2po, k4, yo) to m, sm, k to last 4 sts, yo, k1, yo, k3.

Row 2: K3, yo, p to last 3 sts, yo, k3.

Rep rows 1 and 2, changing to E when you run out of D. When you have enough stitches outside the markers to work another pattern rep, move marker and include these sts in the pattern section. Cont as set until you have 426 sts: 34 x 12-st patt reps and 9 sts at beg and end of row, ending on a WS row.

SET GARTER CHEVRON PATTERN

Row 1 (RS): K3, yo, k to m, sm, (k1, yo, k4, sk2po, k4, yo) to m, sm, k to last 3 sts, yo, k3.

Row 2: Knit.

Rep these 2 rows once more, then row 1 again.

Cast off kwise on WS.

TO FINISH

Weave in ends (see page 71). Block to open out lace pattern (see page 23).

LOVE TRIANGLE SHAWL

A FEW SIMPLE EYELET PATTERNS CAN BE EXTRAORDINARILY EFFECTIVE, AS SHOWN IN THIS STRAIGHTFORWARD TRIANGLE SHAWL IN A GORGEOUSLY LIGHTWEIGHT COTTON BLEND OMBRÉ YARN.

ABOUT THIS YARN

German brand Rico has created a whole range of colour-changing yarn cakes that are a delight to knit with and affordable too. This shawl will work in any of Rico's DK-weight Creative Degradé yarns, but check the length if you do swap in an alternative yarn.

TECHNIQUES

Casting on – page 18
Knit stitch – page 20
Purl stitch – page 21
Stitch markers – page 47
Yarn overs – page 38
Decreasing – page 32
Knitting through the back loop – page 31
Casting off – page 22

SIZE

Width: 69in (175cm)
Depth: 32¼in (82cm)

TENSION

23 sts and 34 rows to 4in (10cm) over st st. *Use larger or smaller needles if necessary to obtain correct tension.*

YOU WILL NEED

Rico Creative Cotton Degradé
50% cotton, 50% acrylic (approx 875yd/800m per 200g)
1 x 200g cake in 01 White/Beige
4mm (UK8:US6) needles
Note: Yarn amounts are based on average requirements and are approximate.

ABBREVIATIONS

See page 148.

LACE TRIANGLES 1

Worked over 11 sts + 5
Row 1: *K6, yo, ssk, k3; rep from * to last 5 sts, k5.
Row 2 and every alt row: Purl.
Row 3: *K5, (yo, ssk) twice, k2; rep from * to last 5 sts, k5.
Row 5: *K4, (yo, ssk) 3 times, k1; rep from * to last 5 sts, k5.
Row 7: *K3, (yo, ssk) 4 times; rep from * to last 5 sts, k5.
These 8 rows form patt and are repeated.
Row 8: Purl.

LACE TRIANGLES 2

Worked over 11 sts + 5
Row 1: K5, *k3, yo, ssk, k6; rep from * to end.
Row 2 and every alt row: Purl.
Row 3: K5, *k2, (yo, ssk) twice, k5; rep from * to end.

Row 5: K5, *k1, (yo, ssk) 3 times, k4; rep from * to end.
Row 7: K5, *(yo, ssk) 4 times, k3; rep from * to end.
These 8 rows form patt and are repeated.
Row 8: Purl.

ZIGZAG LACE

Worked over 8 sts + 1
Note: Stitch count changes over pattern.
Row 1: *K5, yo, k2tog, k1; rep from * to last st before m, k1.
Row 2 and every alt row: Purl.
Row 3: *K3, k2tog tbl, yo, k1, yo, k2tog; rep from * to last st before m, k1.
Row 5: K1, *k1, k2tog tbl, yo, k3, yo, k2tog; rep from * to m.
Row 7: *Yo, k2tog tbl, put st back on LH needle and pass next st on LH needle over it, put st back on RH needle, yo, k5; rep from * to last st before m, k1.
Row 9: *K1, kfb, k6; rep from * to last st before m, k1.
Row 11: *K2tog, k4, yo, k2tog, k1; rep from * to last st before m, k1.
Row 12: Purl.

SHAWL

Pulling your yarn from the centre of the cake (where it is white) cast on 9 sts.

SET-UP

Row 1 (RS): K3, pm, k3, pm, k3.

Row 2: K2, p1, sm, k3, sm, p1, k2.

STOCKING STITCH SECTION

Row 1 (inc): K2, yo, k to m, yo, sm, k3, sm, yo, k to last 2 sts, yo, k2 (4 sts increased).

Row 2: K2, p to m, sm, k3, sm, p to last 2 sts, k2.

Rep last 2 rows until you have 105 sts (2 sts in each g st border, 49 sts in each st st panel, 3 sts in g st spine).

LACE TRIANGLES SECTION 1

Row 1 (set-up): K2, yo, pm, work Lace Triangles 1 patt row 1 to spine m, pm, yo, sm, k3, sm, yo, pm, work Lace Triangles 2 patt row 1 to last 2 sts, pm, yo, k2 (109 sts: 2 sts in each g st border, 51 sts in each st st panel, 3 sts in g st spine).

Row 2: K2, p to spine m, sm, k3, sm, p to last 2 sts, k2.

Row 3: K2, yo, k to m, sm, work next row of Lace Triangles 1 patt to m, sm, k to spine m, yo, sm, k3, sm, yo, k to m, sm, work next row of Lace Triangles 2 patt to m, sm, k to last 2 sts, yo, k2 (113 sts: 2 sts in each g st border, 53 sts in each st st panel, 3 sts in g st spine). The last two rows set Lace Triangles patt. Cont as set until one 8-row patt rep is complete, ending with row 8 of patt (121 sts: 2 sts in each g st border, 57 sts in each panel, 3 sts in g st spine). Remove 4 lace patt markers but not 2 spine markers.

Work 2 rows of st st section until you have 153 sts (2 sts in each g st border, 73 sts in each panel, 3 sts in g st spine).

ZIGZAG LACE SECTION 1

**Row 1 (set-up): K2, yo, pm, work Zigzag Lace row 1 to spine m, pm, yo, sm, k3, sm, yo, pm, work Zigzag Lace row 1 to last 2 sts, pm, yo, k2 (157 sts:

2 sts in each g st border, 75 sts in each panel, 3 sts in g st spine).

Row 2: K2, p to spine m, sm, k3, sm, p to last 2 sts, k2.

Row 3: K2, yo, k to m, sm, work next row of Zigzag Lace to m, sm, k to spine m, yo, sm, k3, sm, yo, k to m, sm, work next row of Zigzag Lace to m, sm, k to last 2 sts, yo, k2 (4 sts increased).

Rows 2 and 3 set position of Zigzag Lace and increases.

Cont as set until one 12-row patt rep of Zigzag Lace is complete, then work rows 3 to 10 again (211 sts: 2 sts in each g st border, 102 sts in each panel, 3 sts in g st spine).

SET NEW POSITION FOR ZIGZAG LACE

Next row (set-up): K2, yo, k2, move panel beg marker to this point, *k5, yo, k2tog, k1*, work row 11 of Zigzag Lace to last st before m, work from * to * removing next m when you come to it, k1, pm, k2, yo, sm, k3, sm, yo, k2, move panel beg marker to this point, work from * to *, work row 11 of Zigzag Lace to last st before m, work from * to * removing next m when you come to it, k1, pm, k2, yo, k2. **

Following the patt set by rows 2 and 3 above, with new position for Zigzag Lace, cont as now set, working rows 2–8 of Zigzag Lace patt (209 sts: 2 sts in each g st border, 101 sts in each panel, 3 sts in g st spine).

Remove 4 panel markers but not 2 spine markers.

Work 2 rows of st st section 7 times until you have 237 sts (2 sts in each g st border, 115 sts in each panel, 3 sts in g st spine).

LACE TRIANGLES SECTION 2

Work Lace Triangles section as above until one 8-row patt rep is complete (253 sts: 2 sts in each g st border, 123 sts in each panel, 3 sts in g st spine).

Work 2 rows of st st section until you have 281 sts (2 sts in each g st border, 137 sts in each panel, 3 sts in g st spine).

ZIGZAG LACE SECTION 2

Work as for section 1 from ** to **, then work rows 2–12 once more as now set, then rows 3–10 again (399 sts: 2 sts in each g st border, 196 sts in each panel, 3 sts in g st spine).

SET NEW POSITION FOR ZIGZAG LACE

Next row (set-up): K2, yo, k4, move panel beg marker to this point, *k5, yo, k2tog, k1*, work Zigzag Lace row 11 to 1 st before m, work from * to * removing next m when you come to it, k1, pm, k to last st before m, yo, sm, k3, sm, yo, k4, move panel beg marker to this point, work from * to *, work Zigzag Lace row 11 to 1 st before m, work from * to * removing next m when you come to it, k1, pm, k to last 2 sts, yo, k2.

Cont in patt as now set, working rows 2 to 8 of Zigzag Lace patt (377 sts: 2 sts in each g st border, 185 sts in each panel, 3 sts in g st spine).

Remove panel markers but not spine markers.

Work 2 rows of st st section until you have 389 sts (2 sts in each g st border, 191 sts in each panel, 3 sts in g st spine).

SET G ST BORDER

Row 1: K2, yo, k to spine m, yo, sm, k3, sm, yo, k to last 2 sts, yo, k2 (4 sts increased).

Row 2: Knit.

Rep these 2 rows until you have 417 sts (2 sts in each g st border, 205 sts in each panel, 3 sts in g st spine).

Cast off very loosely.

TO FINISH

Weave in ends (see page 71).
Block to measurements (see page 23) following the ball band instructions.

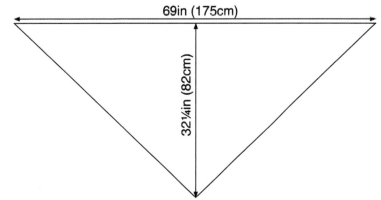

EMBROIDER ON KNITTING

Work a relaxing TV knit, then add a flourish with colourful embroidery.

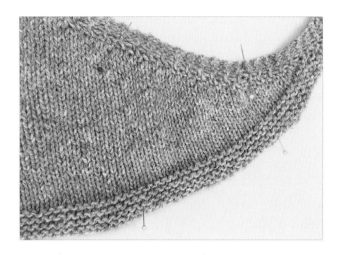

1 Mark the points you want to embroider using pins.

2 In this knit, because of the unusual shape, I traced a pin along the line of knit stitches to mark both ends of the line I wanted to embroider, using the pin end so as not to catch on the wool.

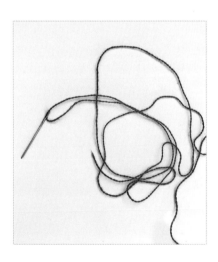

3 Thread a length of yarn on to a blunt-ended yarn needle. This will be a shorter length for the short ends of the shawl and a longer length for the middle.

4 Start off by inserting the needle at the same point as the pin, then remove the pin once you have got the needle to the correct point.

5 Keeping the needle at the correct point, bring it through the fabric from wrong side to right side, leaving a tail about 6in (15cm) long.

6 Insert the needle from right side to wrong side under the next two stitches, then *bring it to the right side again and pull the yarn through.

7 Take the needle back over those two stitches and push it back through the fabric from right side to wrong side at the point where it originally emerged, creating an embroidery stitch on the front of the fabric across two knitted stitches.

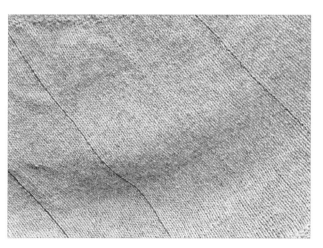

8 Bring the needle from wrong side to right side through the fabric two stitches up, where it originally emerged, then take it from right side to wrong side two further stitches up*, creating a second stitch. Repeat from * to * until a line of stitches runs from the shawl's bottom border to its top edge.

9 Repeat until you have completed your rainbow, using the images in the pattern as a guide, or as desired. Weave in ends on the wrong side.

RAINBOW SHAWL

EMBROIDERY IS A FANTASTIC WAY TO ADD INTERESTING DETAILS AND PERSONALIZATION TO A SHAWL AFTER YOU'VE FINISHED KNITTING. IT ALSO MEANS THAT YOU CAN REALLY RELAX WITH A SIMPLE DESIGN, ALL THE WAY FROM CAST ON TO CAST OFF.

ABOUT THIS YARN
Rauwerk wool comes from a single flock of organically raised German Merino sheep. This woollen-spun, rustic yarn is a different kettle of fish from the smooth, established Merino you thought you knew.

TECHNIQUES
Casting on – page 18
Knit stitch – page 20
Purl stitch – page 21
Increasing – page 30
Decreasing – page 32
Casting off – page 22
Embroider on knitting – page 62

SIZE
Width: approx 83in (210cm)
Long lower edge: approx 66in (168cm)
Short lower edge: approx 42½in (108cm)
Depth at deepest point: 23in (58cm)

TENSION
14 sts and 23 rows to 4in (10cm) over st st. *Tension is not critical to this project.*

YOU WILL NEED
Rauwerk Original 100% Bavarian Merino wool (approx 240yd/220m per 100g)
3 x 100g hanks in Kies (A)
Small amounts of 4 ply wool in rainbow colours
Sample shows **John Arbon Knit By Numbers 4 Ply** (100% organically farmed Falkland Merino wool)
25g mini-skeins in shades 19, 13, 49, 68, 37, 31, 25 and 62
5.5mm (UK5:US9) needles
Tapestry needle
Stitch markers

Note: Yarn amounts are based on average requirements and are approximate.

ABBREVIATIONS
See page 148.

SHAWL
Cast on 5 sts in A.
Knit 2 rows.
Next row: K1, m1L, k1, m1L, k3 (7 sts).

Next row: K2, k2tog, k3 (6 sts).
Next row: K2, m1L, k1, m1L, k3 (8 sts).
Next row: K3, k2tog, k3 (7 sts).
Next row: K3, m1L, k1, m1L, k3 (9 sts).
Next row: K3, p1, p2tog, k3 (8 sts).
SET MAIN PATTERN
Row 1 (RS): K to last 4 sts, m1L, k1, m1L, k3 (inc 2).
Row 2: K3, p to last 5 sts, p2tog, k3 (dec 1).
Note: Stitch count increases by 1 over each 2-row rep.
Rep these 2 rows 131 times (140 sts).

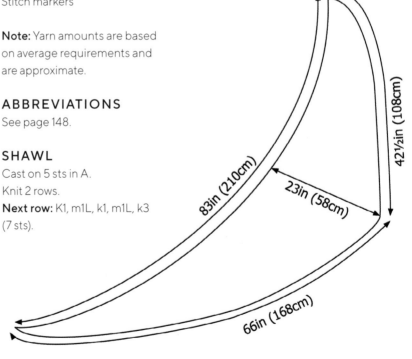

Piece meas approx 66in (168cm) from cast-on edge, measured along shorter shawl border.

Note: You can adjust the length of the shawl to make it shorter or longer by working fewer or more repeats of the main pattern before switching to the border pattern. If you make the shawl longer you may well need more yarn.

SET BORDER

Row 1 (RS): As row 1 above.
Row 2: K to last 5 sts, k2tog, k3.
Rep rows 1 and 2 three more times (144 sts).
Cast off loosely kwise.

TO FINISH

Weave in ends (see page 71).
Block (see page 23).

EMBROIDERY

Using contrast colours as desired, embroider rows of stitches using image as a guide, or in the way you choose.

TIME TO
EXPLORE

- -

TRY OUT NEW
TECHNIQUES AND
EXPAND YOUR
REPERTOIRE

'A half finished shawl left on the coffee
table isn't a mess; it's an object of art'
STEPHANIE PEARL-McPHEE

THAT LITTLE BIT OF
ME TIME

Taking time out to knit is a wonderful way to give yourself a little treat.

What's your ultimate treat? For a big birthday, mine would be a glass of Champagne at Europe's longest wine bar before hopping on a train for a break somewhere exciting. At Christmas my best friends and I like to shop, spa and then drink cocktails served with dry ice pouring out everywhere like a 1980s discotheque. And if my husband and I could go on our dream date, it would be to watch a classic film at a retro, independent cinema and then sit by a fire in a cosy pub and relive every frame.

But life can be busy and tough and I love to give myself everyday treats too. A half hour of yoga first thing really sets me up for the day. In the evening I love to watch something romantic on the TV with some really dark chocolate and a huge mug of peppermint tea. But nothing is quite like the treat of knitting.

The treat can start with an idea – something you'd love to knit, a pattern you've seen or one you've only imagined. Then you can have the joy of searching for it on Ravelry, or even creating it yourself if you're brave enough. Then you buy the wool to match and can knit and knit until you have the wonderful item you envisaged in the first place.

Or the treat could start with a skein of yarn. One you spot in a yarn shop, or at a fibre festival. It's sitting there surrounded by all sorts of other tantalising yarns, but this one stands out. This one demands to be taken home, so you do. Sometimes it will come wrapped in tissue paper and packed in a pretty bag, so that even though you chose it for yourself you can open it like a present, which is after all what it is – your gift to yourself. You might wind this skein straight away – or you might let it sit for days, weeks, months or even years, waiting for it to tell you what it is going to become. And then when it finally does, you'll have the joy of casting on and watching your beautiful yarn unfurl into a wonderful project.

But that's just the big picture. A treat doesn't have to be about going out and spending money (although that can be a great pleasure!). A treat to yourself can be as small as a five-minute screen break during which you knit a couple of rows. Ten minutes to sit in the garden and meditate as you craft. Half an hour in front of your favourite TV show with some soothing stocking stitch. Each time you do it, you'll feel the softness of the yarn moving through your hands, flow with the rhythm of the stitches and notice that tiny bit of progress that can make you feel so good.

Knitting is the treat you can give yourself any time you have a down moment. Do you, like me, live with small, crazy children? Once they reach a certain age you might be able to sneak off and do a row while they're in the bath, or even sit in the park and knit while they play. Do you commute? Your knitting can be with you to pleasantly fill those in-between minutes and hours, and can even ease your mind through frustrating delays. If your career has you stuck to a computer screen for days on end, knitting could be the perfect rest for your eyes when they're tired of the glare.

For those with less frantic lives, knitting is something to pick up and achieve when there's little else to do – or a displacement activity when there's something on the agenda you don't want to tackle right now. If you're feeling lonely it can be a treat to knit something for others, stitching love and connection into each row. In short, it is the gift you can give yourself any time, any place, anywhere – and it just keeps on giving.

FINISHING

When you come to the end of the delightful knitting part of a project, chances are you may have to sew it up and weave in those little ends of yarn that are hanging off it. There are only a couple of projects in this book that need sewing, but each one will leave you with ends to weave into the fabric at the end. Here's all you need to know to sew and finish off as invisibly as possible.

JOINING PIECES WITH MATTRESS STITCH

1 Start with your two finished pieces next to each other, right sides up. Thread a large-eyed, blunt-ended needle with a long piece of yarn. Use the yarn you knitted with – if possible a yarn tail.

2 Insert the needle tip into the stitch at the very left edge of the right-hand fabric from the right side to the wrong side, take it under two bars of stitches and bring it back through the right side and pull through.

3 Repeat step 2 on the left-hand fabric. Move back to the right-hand fabric and repeat step 2 with the next two stitches up. Then do the same with the corresponding stitches on the left-hand side.

4 Pull the yarn through and tighten it. You now have a neat join that is almost invisible on the right side...

5 ...and a neat seam is showing on the wrong side.

TOP TIP
If you're working with chunky yarn or want to achieve an even less visible effect, split your yarn end into two parts and weave each half in separately. The thinner strands will show less than a thick one would.

WEAVING IN ENDS

1 When you come to the end of a project, you'll have a number of ends waiting to be woven in on the wrong side of the work. Choose a large-eyed tapestry needle – blunt or sharp tips should work equally well. With the wrong side facing (in the case of a stocking-stitch project, that's the purl side), thread a yarn end through the eye of the needle. The back of the work is made up of a series of curved stitches: I will call them bowls (which dip downwards) and hats (which curve upwards). Starting with the stitch next to your loose end, insert your needle first underneath the hat next to it, then, following the stitch already running through those loops, upwards through the bowl above it on the right-hand side. Miss out the next hat, upwards and to the left of your working yarn.

2 Insert the needle downwards and to the right into the next bowl to the left of your working yarn, and then through the hat beneath and to the right of it.

3 Miss out the next bowl, then insert your needle upwards and to the right, as in step 1.

4 Repeat steps 1–3 until you have a row of stitches duplicating the stitches in the knitting and neatly securing the loose end. Keep checking that your stitches aren't showing on the right side of the work.

5 Your weaving should be completely invisible on the right side, and the fabric remains nice and stretchy.

SPARKLE AND SHINE
COWL

IF YOU'RE LOOKING FOR A LITTLE TREAT AND A PICK-ME-UP, THIS COWL IS THE PERFECT KNIT. THE ULTIMATE SOFTNESS OF ALPACA, SILK AND CASHMERE WILL SOOTHE YOUR HANDS AS YOU KNIT, AND YOUR HEART WILL BE LIFTED BY THE GENTLE SPARKLE OF THIS DELIGHTFUL LACE-WEIGHT YARN. THEN YOU CAN WRAP THE COWL ROUND AND ROUND YOUR NECK OR LET IT HANG LOOSE ON WARMER DAYS, TO LOOK AND FEEL FABULOUS ALL YEAR ROUND.

ABOUT THIS YARN

This soft lace-weight fibre, exclusive to Richmond yarn boutique Tribe Yarns, is a real luxury to knit with – alpaca, silk, cashmere and just a touch of sparkle.

TECHNIQUES

Holding yarn double – page 77
Slipknot – page 17
Knit stitch – page 20
Purl stitch – page 21
Yarn overs – page 38
Decreasing – page 32
Mattress stitch – page 70

SIZE

Circumference: 59in (150cm)
Depth: 10½in (27cm)

TENSION

22 sts and 24 rows to 4in (10cm) over patt with yarn held double. *Use larger or smaller needles if necessary to obtain correct tension.*

YOU WILL NEED

Tribe Yarns Sparkle Angel Lace
65% baby alpaca, 20% silk, 10% cashmere, 5% Stellina (approx 875yd/300m per 100g)
1 x 100g hank in undyed
4.5mm (UK7:US7) needles

Note: Yarn amounts given are based on average requirements and are approximate.

ABBREVIATIONS

See page 148.

SPECIAL ABBREVIATIONS

kyok = k1, yo, k1 all into next st (inc 2)
sssk = slip 3 sts one at a time kwise, then ktog tbl (dec 2)

PATTERN NOTE

The cowl is knitted with two strands of yarn held together. You may wish to wind your yarn into two balls, or pull yarn from both the outside and the centre of the ball at the same time. Take care not to get your yarn tangled.

COWL

With two strands of yarn held together, make a slipknot.
Row 1: Kyok (3 sts).
Row 2 and all alt rows: Purl.
Row 3: (K1, yo) twice, k1 (5 sts).
Row 5: K2, yo, k1, yo, k2 (7 sts).
Row 7: K3, yo, k1, yo, k3 (9 sts).
SET INCREASE SECTION
Row 1 (RS): K3, yo, k to last 3 sts, yo, k3 (inc 2).

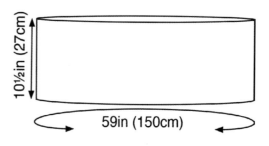

Row 2 and all alt rows: Purl.
Rep rows 1 and 2 three more times
(inc 8 over last 8 rows).
Row 9: K3, yo, k1, (yo, k2tog) to last
3 sts, yo, k3 (inc 2).
Row 10: Purl.
Rep these 10 rows 6 more times,
ending with row 10 (79 sts).

SET STRAIGHT SECTION
Row 1 (RS): K3, yo, k to last 4 sts,
k2tog, k2.
Row 2 and all alt rows: Purl.
Rep rows 1 and 2 three more times.
Row 9: K3, yo, k1, (yo, k2tog) to last
5 sts, yo, k3tog, k2.
Row 10: Purl.

These 10 rows form main patt.
Rep these 10 rows 24 times.
Piece meas 59in (150cm) along
longer edge.

SET DECREASE SECTION
Row 1: K2, ssk, k to last 4 sts, k2tog,
k2 (dec 2).
Row 2 and all alt rows: Purl.
Rep rows 1 and 2 three more times
(total dec 8 sts over 8 rows).
Row 9: K2, ssk, (yo, k2tog) to last
5 sts, yo, k3tog, k2 (dec 2).
Row 10: Purl.
Rep these 10 rows 6 more times,
ending with row 10 (9 sts).
Next row: K3, k3tog, k3 (7 sts).

Next row: Purl.
Next row: K1, ssk, k1, k2tog, k1 (5 sts).
Next row: K1, k3tog, k1 (3 sts).
Next row: Purl.
Next row: K3tog, fasten off.

TO FINISH
Join the two short edges of the cowl
using mattress stitch.
Weave in ends (see page 71).
Block if necessary (see page 23).

GARTER STITCH STRIPES

This pretty textured stripe pattern, made from diluted garter stitch, has to be worked using a double-pointed or a circular needle. It makes a lovely gentle transition between bigger, solid stripes.

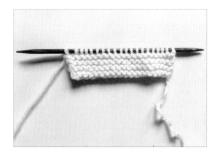

1 Using yarn A, knit the first row, a RS row. At the end of the row do not turn the work, but slide the stitches back to the other end of the circular needle ready to work another RS row.

2 Using yarn B, purl. At the end of this row, turn the work so the WS is facing.

3 Using yarn A, purl. Do not turn the work but again slide the stitches back to the other end of the needle, ready to work the WS again.

4 This time knit the row in B.

5 Repeat these rows to make a pretty textured stripe pattern.

HOLDING YARN DOUBLE

Working with two strands of yarn held together is a great way of blending colours to create a marled effect, mixing different fibres to add textural interest, or simply doubling up a yarn to make it thicker and quicker to knit.

1 Hold the two yarns together as if you were holding only one strand of yarn. Check your yarn balls from time to time to make sure they're not getting tangled.

2 When you come to a stitch made from two strands of yarn, just knit them both together as if it were a single stitch made from just one strand.

PICKING UP STITCHES

Picking up stitches from the edge of knitting is great for adding on neat finishing bands and a way to avoid sewing.

1 With the right side of the fabric facing you and starting in the bottom right-hand corner, *insert the tip of your right-hand needle into the fabric.

2 Pull a loop of working yarn through this hole to create a stitch on your right-hand needle.

3 Repeat from * as directed by your pattern. You can now work these picked-up stitches just like normal stitches.

SKYFALL SHAWL

KITE SHAWLS ARE ONE OF MY FAVOURITE SHAWL TYPES BECAUSE THEY ARE ALWAYS CHANGING AND THEY LOOK SO FABULOUS WHEN THEY'RE DONE. THIS ONE USES SIMPLE COMBINATIONS OF STRIPING, STOCKING STITCH AND GARTER STITCH TO ADD EXTRA INTEREST TO AN ALREADY FABULOUS SHAPE.

ABOUT THIS YARN

Helen Reed of The Wool Kitchen creates a whole world of fantastic colours in her home dye studio in east London. Her soft and lustrous Merino Silk 4 Ply base is a delightful yarn for exploring her inspired colourways, whose brilliant names add extra character to every knit.

TECHNIQUES

Slipknot – page 17
Knit stitch – page 20
Yarn overs – page 38
Knitting through the back loop – page 31
Increasing – page 30
Purl stitch – page 21
Stitch markers – page 47
Garter stitch stripes – page 76
Casting off – page 22

SIZE

Width: 79¼in (201cm)
Deepest depth: 29½in (75cm)

TENSION

23 sts and 31 rows to 4in (10cm) over st st.
Tension is not critical to this project.

YOU WILL NEED

The Wool Kitchen Merino Silk 4 Ply
50% Merino, 50% silk
(approx 437yd/400m per 100g)
1 x 100g hank in Night Swimming (A)
1 x 100g hank in Skyfall (B)
4mm (UK8:US6) circular needle 40in, (100cm) long
Stitch marker

Note: Yarn amounts are based on average requirements and are approximate.

PATTERN NOTE

This design uses nearly all the yarn given in the pattern. If you find you are running out, you may wish to start the double decrease section sooner.

ABBREVIATIONS

See page 148.

SPECIAL ABBREVIATIONS

sk3po = sl1 kwise, k3tog, psso (dec 3)
sp2po = sl1 kwise, p2tog, psso (dec 2)

SHAWL

SET-UP

Using A, make a slipknot.
Row 1 (RS): Knit into the front of the stitch, yo, knit into the back of the stitch (3 sts).
Row 2: Knit.
Row 3: (K1, m1) twice, k1 (5 sts).

Row 4: Knit.
Row 5: K2, yo, k1, yo, k2 (7 sts).
Row 6: K2, yo, p3, yo, k2 (9 sts).
Row 7: K2, yo, k1, pm, sk2po, k1, yo, k2.
Row 8: K2, yo, p to last 2 sts, yo, k2 (11 sts).

DOUBLE INCREASE SECTION

SECTION 1 – ST ST

Row 1 (RS): K2, yo, k to 1 st before m, sl1 kwise, remove marker, k2tog, psso, slip this st back to LH needle, pm, slip st back to RH needle, k to last 2 sts, yo, k2.
Row 2: K2, yo, p to last 2 sts, yo, k2 (13 sts).
Rep these 2 rows 11 more times (35 sts).

SECTION 2 – G ST

Row 1 (RS): As row 1 above.
Row 2: K2, yo, k to 1 st before m, p1, sm, k to last 2 sts, yo, k2 (37 sts).
Rep these 2 rows 2 more times (41 sts).
Work st st section rows 1 and 2, 22 more times (85 sts).
Using B, work section 1, rows 1 and 2, once (87 sts).
Using A work section 1, rows 1 and 2, 15 more times (117 sts).
Using A work section 2, rows 1 and 2, 5 times (127 sts).
Using A work section 1, rows 1 and 2, 10 times (147 sts).
Using B work section 1, rows 1 and 2, twice (151 sts).

SINGLE INCREASE SECTION

Change to A.

SECTION 3 – ST ST

Row 1 (RS): As row 1 above.

Row 2: K2, p to last 2 sts, yo, k2 (152 sts).

Using A, rep last 2 rows 8 more times (160 sts).

Change to B.

SECTION 4 – G ST

Row 1 (RS): As row 1 above.

Row 2: K to 1 st before m, p1, sm, k to last 2 sts, yo, k2 (161 sts).

Rep last 2 rows 2 more times (163 sts).

Using A work section 3, rows 1 and 2, 3 times (166 sts).

Using B work section 3, rows 1 and 2, once (167 sts).

Using A work section 3, rows 1 and 2, twice (169 sts).

Using B work section 3, rows 1 and 2, once (170 sts).

Using A work section 4, rows 1 and 2, 4 times (174 sts).

Using A work section 3, rows 1 and 2, 3 times (177 sts).

SET DILUTED STRIPES

Row 1 (RS): Using A, work as row 1 above. Do not turn, slide sts to other end of needle to work the RS again.

Row 2 (RS): Using B, p2, yo, p to m, sm, k1, p to end (178 sts). Turn.

Row 3 (WS): Using A, p2, yo, p to 2 sts before m, rm, sp2po, pm, p to last 2 sts, yo, p2. Do not turn, slide sts to other end of needle to work the WS again.

Row 4 (WS): Using B, k to 1 st before m, p1, k to last 2 sts, yo, k2 (179 sts). Turn.

Rep these 4 rows 3 more times (185 sts).

Using B work section 3, rows 1 and 2, twice (187 sts).

STRAIGHT SECTION

Cont in B.

SECTION 5 – ST ST

Row 1 (RS): K2, yo, k to 1 st before m, sl1 kwise, remove marker, k2tog, psso, slip st back to LH needle, pm, sl st back to RH needle, k to end.

Row 2: K2, p to last 2 sts, yo, k2.

Rep section 5, rows 1 and 2, two more times.

Using A work section 5, rows 1 and 2, once.

Change to B.

SECTION 6 – G ST

Row 1 (RS): As row 1 in section 5.

Row 2: K to 1 st before m, p1, sm, k to last 2 sts, yo, k2.

Rep last 2 rows 2 more times.

Using B work section 5, rows 1 and 2, 3 times.

Using A work section 5, rows 1 and 2, twice.

Using B work section 5, rows 1 and 2, 4 times.

Using A work section 6, rows 1 and 2, 3 times.

Using B work section 5, rows 1 and 2, 5 times.

Using B work section 6, rows 1 and 2, 4 times.

Using B work section 5, rows 1 and 2, 5 times.

Using A work section 5, rows 1 and 2, once.

Using B work section 5, rows 1 and 2, 4 times.

Using A work section 5, rows 1 and 2, twice.

Using B work section 5, rows 1 and 2, 8 times.

Using B work section 6, rows 1 and 2, 3 times.

Using B work section 5, rows 1 and 2, 10 times.

Using A work section 5, rows 1 and 2, once.

Change to B.

DECREASE SECTION

SECTION 7 – ST ST

Row 1 (RS): K2, yo, k to 1 st before m, sl1 kwise, rm, k3tog, psso, slip st back to LH needle, pm, slip st back to RH needle, k to end.

Row 2: K2, p to last 2 sts, yo, k2 (186 sts).

Rep last 2 rows 2 more times (184 sts).

Cont in B.

SECTION 8 – G ST

Row 1 (RS): As row 1 in section 7.

Row 2: K to 1 st before m, p1, sm, k to last 2 sts, yo, k2 (183 sts).

Rep last 2 rows once more (182 sts).

Using A, work section 8, rows 1 and 2, two more times (180 sts).

Cast off kwise on RS.

TO FINISH

Weave in ends (see page 71).

Block to measurements, using pins to accentuate point of triangle (see page 23).

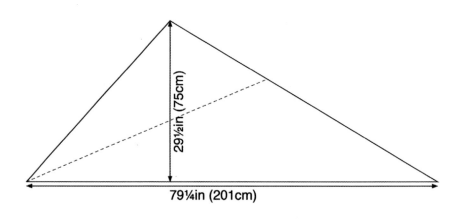

29½in (75cm)

79¼in (201cm)

BUNDLED COWL

HOW DO YOU MAKE A KNITTED COWL EVEN MORE COSY THAN IT IS ALREADY? SEW A COSY FLEECE OR A SOFT BRUSHED COTTON TO THE INSIDE TO LINE IT AND YOU'LL BE COSIER THAN YOU COULD EVER IMAGINE. THIS LITTLE NECK WARMER CAN DOUBLE UP AS A CUTE AND QUIRKY HAT.

ABOUT THIS YARN

Based in Uruguay and Peru, Malabrigo gives work to women who might otherwise struggle to find it. Its super chunky, kettle-dyed Rasta yarn is a buttery-soft treat to work with that will knit up in no time flat.

TECHNIQUES

Casting on – page 18
Knit stitch – page 20
Purl stitch – page 21
Cables – page 36
Casting off – page 22

SIZE

Circumference: 19¾in (50cm)
Depth: 8¾in (22cm)

TENSION

9.5 sts and 12 rnds to 4in (10cm) over rev st st. *Use larger or smaller needles if necessary to obtain correct tension.*

YOU WILL NEED

Malabrigo Rasta 100% kettle-dyed Merino wool (approx 90yd/82m per 150g)
1 x 150g hank in 005 Aniversario
12mm (US17) circular or double-pointed needles
Cable needle
Stitch marker
Pink fleece fabric approx 20½ x 9½in (52 x 24cm)
Sewing needle and matching thread

Note: Yarn amounts are based on average requirements and are approximate.

ABBREVIATIONS

See page 148.

SPECIAL ABBREVIATIONS

Cr3L = cross 3 left: slip next 2 sts on to cn and hold at front, p1, k2 from cn
Cr3R = cross 3 right: slip next st on to cn and hold at back, k2, p1 from cn
Cr5R = cross 5 right: slip next 3 sts on to cn and hold at back, k2, slip last st on cn back to LH needle, bring cn to front, p1 from LH needle, k2 from cn
MB = make bobble: k into front, back, front, then back of next st (4 sts), turn, p4, turn, sl1, k3tog, psso (1 st)

DIAMOND CABLE

Worked over 9 sts and 10 rnds
Rnd 1: P1, k2, p3, k2, p1.
Rnd 2: P1, Cr3L, p1, Cr3R, p1.
Rnd 3 and all foll alt rnds: Work each st as it appears – k the k sts and p the p ones.
Rnd 4: P2, Cr5R, p2.
Rnd 6: P1, Cr3R, p1, Cr3L, p1.
Rnd 8: Cr3R, p1, MB, p1, Cr3L.
Rnd 10: Cr3L, p3, Cr3R.

NECK WARMER

Cast on 40 sts, join to work in the round and pm to mark beg of rnd.
Rnd 1: Knit.
Rnd 2: Purl.
Rep last 2 rnds once more.

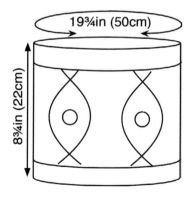

Next rnd (inc): (K4, kfb) around
(48 sts).
SET DIAMOND CABLE PATTERN
Rnd 1: *P3, work rnd 1 of Diamond
Cable patt; rep from * around.
This rnd sets patt. Cont as set until
you have worked one full 10-rnd patt
rep, then rnds 1–7 again.
Next rnd (dec): (K4, k2tog) around
(40 sts).
Next rnd: Purl.
Next rnd: Knit.
Rep last 2 rnds once more.
Cast off.

TO FINISH

Weave in ends (see page 71).
Fold your fleece in half lengthways
with right sides together and sew
a ½in (1cm) seam.
Without reversing the fabric, so the
right sides are still on the inside, insert
the tube you have made into the
inside (WS) of the neck warmer, fold
over ½in (1cm) at each edge and stitch
into place.

JOURNEY SHAWL

ASTAIR MEANS 'JOURNEY' IN GAELIC, AND AS YOU KNIT THIS SHAWL YOU WILL GO ON A VOYAGE DISCOVERING THE NATURAL WOOL SHADES THAT DECORATE THE HEBRIDEAN HILLSIDES.

ABOUT THIS YARN

Uist Wool's Astair is spun on the remote island of Grimsay in North Uist, part of the Outer Hebrides, on heritage machinery that has been saved and rebuilt to make knitting yarn from the fleece of local sheep, bought directly from growers at sustainable prices.

TECHNIQUES

Garter tab cast on – page 50
Knit stitch – page 20
Purl stitch – page 21
Stitch markers – page 47
Yarn overs – page 38
Garter stitch stripes – page 76
Casting off – page 22

SIZE

Width: 63in (160cm)
Depth: 28¼in (72cm)

TENSION

22 sts and 34 rows to 4in (10cm) over st st. *Use larger or smaller needles if necessary to obtain correct tension.*

YOU WILL NEED

Uist Wool Astair
(approx 186–191yd/170–175m per 50g)
1 x 50g hank in Coire – Corrie
(50% white alpaca, 50% white Cheviot wool) (A)
1 x 50g hank in Poll – Fishing Pool
(grey, black and white alpaca and Cheviot wool) (B)
1 x 50g hank in Maol – Flat Hill Top (red alpaca and white Cheviot wool) (C)
1 x 50g hank in Abhainn – River (black alpaca and white Cheviot wool) (D)
1 x 50g hank in Bealach – Mountain Pass (brown alpaca, Moorit Shetland and dark Scottish Merino wool) (E)
1 x 50g hank in Sgeir – Crag (white alpaca and dark Shetland wool) (F)
3.5mm (UK9:US4) circular needle at least 40in (100cm) long
5 stitch markers

Note: Yarn amounts are based on average requirements and are approximate.

ABBREVIATIONS

See page 148.

SECTION 1

Row 1 (RS): K3, (sm, yo, k to 1 st before m, yo, k1) 4 times, sm, k3.
Row 2: K3, p to last 4 sts, k3.
Row 3: Knit.
Row 4: As row 2.

SECTION 2

Row 1 (RS): With first colour work as Section 1 row 1 but do not turn, slide sts back to other end of needle to work RS again.
Row 2 (RS): With second colour p3, (sm, p to 1 st before m, k1) 4 times, sm, p3. Turn work.
Row 3 (WS): With first colour, purl. Do not turn, slide sts back to other end of needle to work WS again.
Row 4 (WS): With second colour, k3, (sm, p1, k to m) 4 times, sm, k3.

SHAWL

GARTER TAB CAST ON

Using A, cast on 3 sts.
Knit 8 rows in g st.
After last row do not turn but rotate work 90 degrees. Pick up 4 sts along long edge of tab, 1 in each g st bump, rotate work 90 degrees again and pick up 3 sts from cast-on edge (10 sts).
Knit 1 row.
Next row (RS): K3, (pm, k1, yo) 4 times, pm, k3.
Next row: K3, p to last 3 sts, k3.
Next row: Knit.
Next row: K3, p to last 3 sts, k3.

SET MAIN PATTERN

Work Section 1 ten times.
**Using A as first colour and B as second colour, work Section 2 once.
Using B, work Section 1 once.

Using B as first colour and A as second colour, work Section 2 once.
Using A, work Section 1 once.
Using A as first colour and B as second colour, work Section 2 once.**
Using B, work Section 1 ten times.
Rep from ** to ** but using B in place of A and C in place of B.
Using C, work Section 1 five times.
Rep from ** to ** but using C in place of A and D in place of B.
Using D, work Section 1 three times.
Using D as first colour and E as second colour, work Section 2 once.
Using E, work Section 1 once.
Using E as first colour and D as second colour, work Section 2 once.
Using D, work section 1 once.
Using F as first colour and E as second colour, work Section 2 once.
Using E, work Section 1 once.
Using E as first colour and F as second colour, work Section 2 once.

Using F, work Section 1 once.
Using F as first colour and E as second colour, work Section 2 once.
Using E, work Section 1 once.
Using E as first colour and F as second colour, work Section 2 once.
Break E and cont in F only, work as foll:
Row 1: Work as row 1 of Section 1.

Rows 2–4: Knit.
Using F as first colour and A as second colour, work Section 2 once.
Cast off in A.

TO FINISH
Weave in ends (see page 71).
Block (see page 23).

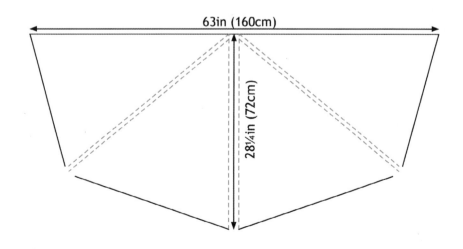

63in (160cm)

28¼in (72cm)

UNWIND SHAWL

THIS DELIGHTFUL KITE SHAWL PLAYS WITH TEXTURE AND OMBRÉ COLOUR GRADIENTS AND GROWS INTO A BEAUTIFULLY ENVELOPING WRAP. DEVONIA 4 PLY IS SPUN AT JOHN ARBON'S MILL IN DEVON, SOUTHWEST ENGLAND, FROM THE BLENDED FLEECE OF LOCAL SHEEP, MAKING THIS A WONDERFUL PROJECT FOR A HOLIDAY IN THE WEST COUNTRY.

ABOUT THIS YARN

Devon-based John Arbon spins this beautifully soft and silky wool from the fleeces of locally raised Exmoor Blueface, Devon Bluefaced Leicester and Devon Wensleydale sheep.

TECHNIQUES

Casting on – page 18
Knit stitch – page 20
Purl stitch – page 21
Yarn overs – page 38
Decreasing – page 32
Stitch markers – page 47
Garter stitch stripes – page 76
Casting off – page 22

SIZE

Width: 91¼in (232cm)
Length: 29½in (75cm)

TENSION

21 sts and 44 rows to 4in (10cm) over g st.
Tension is not critical to this project.

YOU WILL NEED

John Arbon Devonia 4 Ply
50% Exmoor Blueface, 30% Devon Bluefaced Leicester, 20% Devon Wensleydale wool (approx 424yd/388m per 100g)
1 x 100g hank in Devonia Cream (A)
1 x 100g hank in Nightshade (B)
1 x 100g hank in Bleeding Heart (C)
1 x 100g hank in Broken Flower (D)
1 x 100g hank in Cinder Glow (E)
4mm (UK8:US6) circular needle, 40in (100cm) long
Stitch marker

Note: Yarn amounts are based on average requirements and are approximate.

ABBREVIATIONS

See page 148.

SPECIAL ABBREVIATIONS

sp2po = sl1 kwise, p2tog, psso (dec 2)

STRIPE PATTERN

*20 rows A.
8 rows of diluted stripe patt using A and B.
20 rows B.
Rep this patt, switching from B to C, C to D, D to E, E to D*, D to C, C to B and B to A, then rep from * to * again, ending with shade D.

SHAWL

SET-UP
Using A, make a slipknot.
Row 1: Kyok (3 sts).
Row 2: Knit.
Row 3: (K1, m1) twice, k1 (5 sts).
Row 4: Knit.
Row 5: K2, yo, k1, yo, k2 (7 sts).
Row 6: K2, yo, k3, yo, k2 (9 sts).
Row 7: K2, yo, k1, pm, sk2po, k1, yo, k2.
Row 8: K2, yo, k to last 2 sts, yo, k2 (11 sts).

DOUBLE INCREASE SECTION
SECTION 1 – G ST
Row 1 (RS): K2, yo, k to 1 st before m, sl1 kwise, remove m, k2tog, psso, slip st back to LH needle, pm, slip st back to RH needle, k to last 2 sts, yo, k2.
Row 2: K2, yo, k to 1 st before m, p1, sm, k to last 2 sts, yo, k2.
Rep these 2 rows until 20 rows have been worked in A (23 sts).

SECTION 2 – DILUTED STRIPES
Row 1 (RS): Using A, work as row 1 above. At the end of the row do not turn, slide sts back to other end of needle to work RS again.
Row 2 (RS): Using B, p2, yo, p to m, sm, k1, p to last 2 sts, yo, p2. Turn.
Row 3 (WS): Using A, p2, yo, p to 2 sts before m, remove m, sp2po, pm, p to last 2 sts, yo, p2. Do not turn but slide sts back to other end of needle to work WS again.

Row 4 (WS): Using B, k2, yo, k to 1 st before m, p1, sm, k to last 2 sts, k2 (27 sts).

Rep these 4 rows once more (31 sts).

Cont in B only, work g st patt for 20 rows.

Cont as set in stripe patt, working g st and diluted stripe sections as set, until you have worked D–C diluted stripe.

SINGLE INCREASE SECTION

Cont in stripe patt as set, beg with C stripe and working sections 4 and 5 below until you have worked B–A diluted stripe.

SECTION 3 – G ST

Row 1 (RS): As row 1 above.

Row 2: K to 1 st before m, p1, sm, k to last 2 sts, yo, k2 (inc 1).

SECTION 4 – DILUTED STRIPES

Row 1 (RS): Using first colour, work as row 1 above. Do not turn, slide sts to other end of needle to work RS again.

Row 2 (RS): Using second colour, p2, yo, p to m, sm, k1, p to end. Turn.

Row 3 (WS): Using first colour, p2, yo, p to 2 sts before m, remove m, sp2po, pm, p to last 2 sts, yo, p2. Do not turn, slide sts to other end of needle to work WS again.

Row 4 (WS): Using second colour, k to 1 st before m, p1, sm, k to last 2 sts, yo, k2. Turn.

Rep these 4 rows once more (inc 4).

STRAIGHT SECTION

Cont in stripe patt as set, working sections 5 and 6 below until only 2 sts rem after m (1 st after central double decrease).

SECTION 5 – G ST

Row 1 (RS): K2, yo, k to 1 st before m, sl1 kwise, remove m, k2tog, psso, slip st back to LH needle, pm, sl st back to RH needle, k to end.

Row 2: K to 1 st before m, p1, sm, k to last 2 sts, yo, k2.

SECTION 6 – DILUTED STRIPES

Row 1 (RS): Using first colour, work as row 1 in section 5 above. Do not turn, slide sts to other end of needle to work RS again.

Row 2 (RS): Using second colour, p2, yo, p to m, sm, k1, p to end. Turn.

Row 3 (WS): Using first colour, p to 2 sts before m, remove m, sp2po, pm, p to last 2 sts, yo, p2. Do not turn, slide sts to other end of needle to work WS again.

Row 4 (WS): Using second colour, k to 1 st before m, p1, sm, k to last 2 sts, yo, k2.

Rep these 4 rows once more.

TO FINISH

Weave in ends (see page 71).
Block to measurements (see page 23).

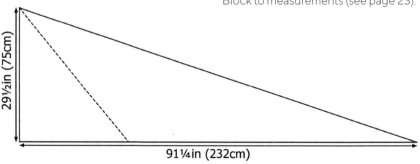

29½in (75cm)

91¼in (232cm)

AFTERGLOW WRAP

THIS COSY, BLANKET-LIKE SUPER SCARF CAN BE WORN IN FOUR DIFFERENT WAYS: AS AN OVERSIZED SCARF, A TRADITIONAL WRAP, BUTTONED INTO A PONCHO OR BUTTONED INTO A WIDE-SLEEVED SHRUG. WITH A GLOWING OMBRÉ EFFECT CREATED BY USING TWO STRANDS OF SUPER-SOFT, LIGHT-AS-A-FEATHER LACE-WEIGHT YARN TOGETHER, IT IS BOTH ELEGANT AND UTTERLY COMFORTING.

ABOUT THIS YARN

Malabrigo is a family-owned company based in Uruguay and Peru, making beautifully soft and vibrant hand-dyed yarns that sell all over the world. The company employs mainly women, particularly those with fewer opportunities than most.

TECHNIQUES

Holding yarn double – page 77
Casting on – page 18
Knit stitch – page 20
Purl stitch – page 21
Yarn overs – page 38
Decreasing – page 32
Casting off – page 22
Picking up stitches – page 77

SIZE

Width: 80in (202cm)
Depth: 27in (68cm)

TENSION

22 sts x 30 rows to 4in (10cm) over patt with yarn held double. *Use larger or smaller needles if necessary to obtain correct tension.*

YOU WILL NEED

Malabrigo Lace 100% wool (470yd/430m per 50g)
2 x 50g hanks in 148 Holly Hock (A)
2 x 50g hanks in 130 Damask (B)
2 x 50g hanks in 17 Pink Frost (C)
2 x 50g hanks in 184 Shocking Pink (D)
2 x 50g hanks in 93 Fucsia (E)
4mm (UK8:US6) needles
16 buttons

Note: Yarn amounts given are based on average requirements and are approximate.

ABBREVIATIONS

See page 148.

WRAP

With 2 strands of A held together, cast on 150 sts.
Work 2 rows in st st.
SET LACE LADDERS PATTERN
Row 1 (RS): K1, (k4, yo, skpo) 24 times, k5.
Row 2 and every alt row: Purl.
Row 3: K1, (k4, k2tog, yo) 24 times, k5.
These 4 rows form lace ladder patt.
Continue in patt until work meas 8¾in (22cm).
Break 1 strand of A and join 1 strand of B so you are holding 1 strand each of A and B.
Continue in patt until work meas 17¼in (44cm).

Break A and join another strand of B so you are holding 2 strands of B.
Continue in patt until work meas 26in (66cm).
Break one strand of B and join 1 strand of C so you are holding 1 strand each of B and C.
Continue in patt until work meas 34¾in (88cm).
Break B and join another strand of C so you are holding 2 strands of C.
Continue in patt until work meas 43¼in (110cm).
Break 1 strand of C and join 1 strand of D so you are holding 1 strand each of C and D.
Continue in patt until work meas 52in (132cm).
Break C and join another strand of D so you are holding 2 strands of D.
Continue in patt until work meas 60¾in (154cm).
Break 1 strand of D and join 1 strand of E so you are holding 1 strand each of D and E.
Continue in patt until work meas 69¼in (176cm).
Break D and join 1 strand of E so you are holding 2 strands of E.
Cont in patt until work meas 78in (198cm).
Work 2 rows in st st.
Cast off loosely.

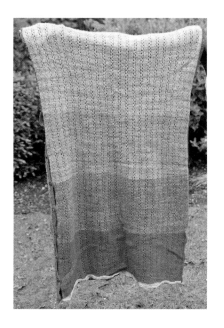 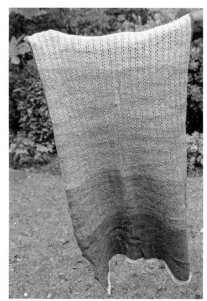 

SIDE BORDERS

With RS facing and 2 strands of E held together, pick up and knit 460 sts along side of wrap.

Row 1: Knit.

Row 2 (buttonhole row): (K18, yo, k2tog) 8 times, k to end.

Knit 2 rows.

Cast off loosely.

Repeat on other side.

END BORDERS

With 2 strands of C held together and RS facing, pick up and knit 190 sts across end of wrap.

Rows 1 and 3 (WS): Purl.

Row 2: Knit.

Row 4: K3, p2tog, *(p2tog) 3 times, (k1, yo) 6 times, (p2tog) 3 times; rep from * to last 5 sts, p2tog, k3 (189 sts).

Row 5: Purl.

Cast off loosely.

Repeat on other side.

TO FINISH

Weave in ends (see page 71). Sew buttons on to side borders to match buttonholes.

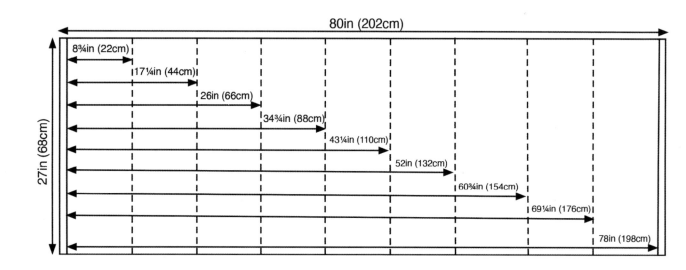

80in (202cm)

27in (68cm)

8¾in (22cm)

17¼in (44cm)

26in (66cm)

34¾in (88cm)

43¼in (110cm)

52in (132cm)

60¾in (154cm)

69¼in (176cm)

78in (198cm)

GIVING **IS LIVING**

The joys and sorrows of knitting for other people...

I love knitting for other people. I love working each stitch, thinking about how it will keep a loved one warm, and look great, and be a reminder of my care and affection when we can't be close. And there's nothing like seeing someone's delight when you give them a knitted present you've thought out carefully, worked hard on and then wrapped up ready to hand it over.

But sometimes it doesn't quite work out that way. The first jumper I ever knitted for my husband came out with a neck that looked like an Elizabethan ruff. Still he wore it faithfully, accepting it for the love woven into the stitches rather than for the dubious fashion sense. A good friend was made a tote bag with Bob Dylan's face in Fair Isle knitting emblazoned across it. But the face came out so squashed I had to send it with a note explaining who it was meant to be.

Then there are the times when the gift doesn't go down so well. I'll never forget the mortification of the morning I visited a very hungover friend the day after a big birthday celebration. She held up a snood I had made for her and said, with a mixture of disgust and disbelief: 'And someone gave me *this*!' Then there are things my kids have asked me for – like the double-knitted Hogwarts scarf I laboured over for my son, which he never wears. And the jumper with intarsia flame sleeves he asked for, which he never wears. Sometimes it's not even the recipient's fault – one much-loved, all-over lace-patterned hat in 4 ply pure alpaca was eaten by its owner's dog, something that still makes me feel slightly sick given how much time I put into it. Other things are worked over, given with love, received with apparent joy – and never seen again.

But that's not the point.

When we knit for others it's not really about giving them something that is exactly what they want. They could get that for themselves if we gave them the cash instead, it would probably cost less money and certainly less time and effort. If we really loved them we might even give them the yarn and needles so they could have the joy of knitting themselves.

There are two things at play when we give knitted gifts. The first is to give someone a unique present they couldn't get from anyone else, something that shows them how special they are, by including not only your money but also your time and your effort and your love. The second is a gift to ourselves – after all, we get to knit it.

At best, knitted gifts become treasured heirlooms, reminding us of the maker for the rest of our lives. My husband and I were given a granny square blanket for our wedding. It took our friend a full series of TV's *24* to make it for us (which just goes to show how long ago it was) and it has been on our bed ever since. When we have moved house, it has been the arrival of that blanket that has turned the new place into a home.

And there's nothing like seeing a knitted gift that is being worn and used and loved. Like the wedding shawl I knitted for my best friend, which she then wrapped her twin baby girls in when they were born. And the mermaid tail I made my daughter, which she loves to cuddle up in. I love it when I'm out for a walk with a friend and they pull a pair of mittens I've made for them out of their pockets, not for my benefit but because that is the pair they like to have with them all the time. It just makes it all worthwhile.

Because I knit so much myself, I treasure hand-knitted gifts more than ever – after all, I know what goes into them.

IT'S A SHAWL THING

Shawls make marvellous gifts. They fit everyone, they can be for any season, they're perfect for layering and the bigger ones can double up as lap blankets for snuggling up on the sofa. But they're big projects, and they tend to take longer than we think they will. So choose your victim well, think hard about what they would like to wear and you would like to make – and only knit them a shawl if you really love them.

UNDERSTANDING CHARTS

Don't be daunted by charted knitting instructions – once you understand how to read them they can be very straightforward and can really help with your knitting.

Reading charts can appear really daunting, but many knitters swear by them. In Japan, knitting patterns are written solely in charts, and fans of Japanese patterns insist that non-Japanese-speaking knitters can understand them with just a technique decoder, saying they are more straightforward than written patterns. For many years I only used charts for colourwork patterns, where they are essential – who can cope with 'knit one stitch in A, knit three stitches in B' and so on? But recently, I've come to find charts help with all sorts of stitch patterns, especially lace and cables.

TOP TIPS

- Start with the key: there are standard chart symbols, but they are not universal, so always read the key carefully before embarking on a chart.
- Read the written pattern as well – often a charted pattern will be set within a written pattern. It's always a good idea to read all the way through a pattern before casting on, to work out exactly where your chart is placed.
- Is the project knitted back and forth, with the right side and wrong side facing you alternately – or in the round, with only the right side facing? Flat-knitted charts are read first from right to left, usually on odd-numbered, right-side rows, then from left to right. When knitting in the round, read every row from right to left.
- Count your stitches carefully – if you get the number of plain stitches before a yarn over or a decrease wrong you could find yourself way off across the row or round.
- It may be helpful to place stitch markers to mark the placement of the charted section, or in between pattern repeats.

BEDTIME WRAP CHART (see page 44)

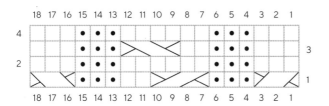

KEY

▢ RS: knit, WS: purl

• RS: purl, WS: knit

⟋⟍ C3B

⟍⟋ C3F

⟋⟍ C4B

⟍⟋ C4F

WEDDING WRAP CHART (see page 100)

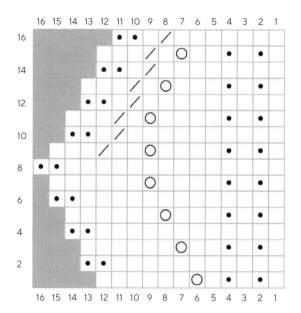

KEY

☐ RS: knit, WS: purl	▨ no stitch
• RS: purl, WS: knit	╱ RS: k2tog, WS: p2tog
◯ yo	

HAP-PINESS HAP CHART (see page 130)

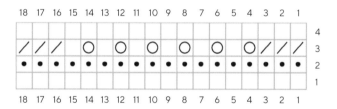

KEY

☐	knit
•	purl
╱	k2tog
◯	yo

WEDDING WRAP

THIS DESIGN IS BASED ON A WRAP I KNITTED MY BEST FRIEND FOR HER BONFIRE NIGHT WEDDING
A FEW YEARS AGO, WITH A DELICATE LACE EDGE AND A COSY STOCKING STITCH CENTRE. A COUPLE
OF YEARS AFTER THE WEDDING SHE HAD TWIN BABY GIRLS, AND SHE WRAPPED THE LITTLE ONES UP
IN HER WEDDING SHAWL IN THEIR MOSES BASKET. IN A GLORIOUS BLEND OF ALPACA AND COTTON,
THIS VERSATILE WRAP MAKES A WONDERFUL GIFT.

ABOUT THIS YARN

British yarn brand Rowan has been leading the way in knitwear and yarn design since it was founded in Yorkshire in 1978. Alpaca Classic is a blend of alpaca and cotton that is light, feathery and very warm, and it comes in a wide range of inspiring colours.

TECHNIQUES

Casting on – page 18
Knit stitch – page 20
Purl stitch – page 21
Yarn overs – page 38
Decreasing – page 32
Stitch markers – page 47
Casting off – page 22

SIZE

Width: 63in (160cm)
Depth: 19¾in (50cm)

TENSION

18 sts x 34 rows to 4in (10cm) over st st. *Use larger or smaller needles if necessary to obtain correct tension.*

YOU WILL NEED

Rowan Alpaca Classic 57% alpaca, 43% cotton (approx 131yd/120m per 25g)
8 x 25g balls in 115 Snowflake White
3.5mm (UK9:US4) needles
Stitch markers

Note: Yarn amounts given are based on average requirements and are approximate.

ABBREVIATIONS

See page 148.

MAIN LACE AND RIB PATT

Worked over 14 sts and 16 rows
Row 1 (RS): (K1, p1) twice, k1, yo, k3, sk2po, k3, yo.
Row 2 and all alt rows: Purl.
Row 3: (K1, p1) twice, k2, yo, k2, sk2po, k2, yo, k1.
Row 5: (K1, p1) twice, k3, yo, k1, sk2po, k1, yo, k2.
Row 7: (K1, p1) twice, k4, yo, sk2po, yo, k3.
Row 9: As row 7.
Row 11: As row 5.
Row 13: As row 3.
Row 15: As row 1.
Row 16: Purl.

RIGHT EDGE PATT

Note: Stitch count changes over patt but starts and ends with 11 sts. When worked with main lace patt, stop patt at * on RS rows and move to main lace patt. On WS rows start patt from * where marked.
Row 1 (RS): K6, yo*, (k1, p1) twice, k1.
Rows 2, 4, 6 and 8: P to last 2 sts, k2.
Row 3: K6, yo, k1*, (k1, p1) twice, k1.
Row 5: K6, yo, k2*, (k1, p1) twice, k1.
Row 7: K6, yo, k3*, (k1, p1) twice, k1.
Row 9: K3, ssk, k2, yo, k3*, (k1, p1) twice, k1.
Row 10: P5, *p5, p2tog tbl, p1, k2.
Row 11: K3, ssk, k1, yo, k3*, (k1, p1) twice, k1.
Row 12: P5, *p4, p2tog tbl, p1, k2.
Row 13: K3, ssk, k1, yo, k2*, (k1, p1) twice, k1.
Row 14: P5, *p3, p2tog tbl, p1, k2.
Row 15: K3, ssk, k1, yo, k1*, (k1, p1) twice, k1.
Row 16: P5, *p2, p2tog tbl, p1, k2.

LEFT EDGE PATT

Note: Stitch count changes over patt but starts and ends with 11.
Row 1 (RS): (K1, p1) twice, k1, yo, k6.
Rows 2, 4, 6 and 8: K2, p to end.
Row 3: (K1, p1) twice, k2, yo, k6.
Row 5: (K1, p1) twice, k3, yo, k6.
Row 7: (K1, p1) twice, k4, yo, k6.

KNITTED SHAWLS

LEFT EDGE PATTERN

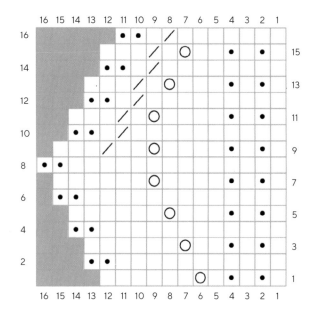

KEY

	RS: knit, WS: purl		no stitch
•	RS: purl, WS: knit	/	RS: k2tog, WS: p2tog
O	yo		

RIGHT EDGE PATTERN

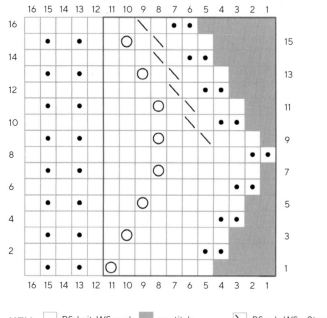

KEY

	RS: knit, WS: purl		no stitch	\	RS: ssk, WS: p2tog tbl
O	yo	•	RS: purl, WS: knit		Border repeat

MAIN LACE PATTERN

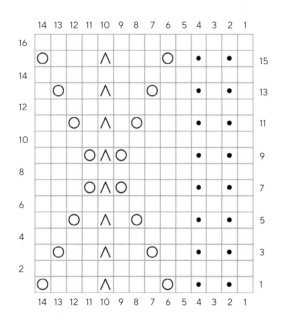

KEY

	RS: knit, WS: purl	O	yo
•	RS: purl, WS: knit	∧	sk2po

19¾in (50cm)

63in (160cm)

Row 9: (K1, p1) twice, k4, yo, k2, k2tog, k3.

Row 10: K2, p1, p2tog, p10.

Row 11: (K1, p1) twice, k4, yo, k1, k2tog, k3.

Row 12: K2, p1, p2tog, p9.

Row 13: (K1, p1) twice, k3, yo, k1, k2tog, k3.

Row 14: K2, p1, p2tog, p8.

Row 15: (K1, p1) twice, k2, yo, k1, k2tog, k3.

Row 16: K2, p1, p2tog, p7.

WRAP

Cast on 115 sts.

Knit 2 rows.

SET BORDER PATT

**Row 1 (RS): Work row 1 of Right Edge Patt to *, work row 1 of 14-st Main Lace Patt 7 times, work row 1 of Left Edge Patt.

Row 2: Work row 2 of Left Edge Patt, work row 2 of Main Lace Patt 6 times, work row 2 of Right Edge Patt from * to end.

These 2 rows set border patt. Cont as set until you have worked row 16.
**

Piece meas approx 2¼in (5.5cm) at points and 1½in (4cm) in dips.

SET MAIN PATT

Row 1 (RS): Work row 1 of Right Edge Patt (12 sts), pm1, k to last 12 sts, pm2, work row 1 of Left Edge Patt (12 sts).

Row 2: Work row 2 of Left Edge Patt, sm2, p to m, sm1, work row 2 of Right Edge Patt.

These 2 rows set main patt, with 12 sts in Edge Patt at each edge, and st st between markers.

Cont as set until piece meas approx 61½in (156cm).

SET END BORDER

Work as for start border from ** to **.

Knit 2 rows.

Cast off loosely.

TO FINISH

Weave in ends (see page 71).

Block firmly (see page 23) to open out lace pattern, using pins to accentuate the points, especially on cast-off edge where they are less pronounced.

ELONGATED STITCHES

Don't scream – we drop elongated stitches to create the Sea Foam Wave pattern on page 106. Elongating stitches creates a striking lacy, openwork effect, but dropping them off the needle can be scary! Brace yourself and learn how to do it.

1 The Sea Foam Wave pattern in the Sea Foam Shawlette on page 106 is worked across 10 sts plus six and starts with a right-side knit row. Here I am working two repeats of the pattern.

2 On the second row, a wrong-side row, start by knitting 6 sts, then *work 'yo, k1' as you would for a normal lace eyelet.

3 Before the next stitch, take the yarn over to the back of the needle, bring it between the two needle tips to the front, then take it over to the back again, creating a double yarn over.

4 After the next knit stitch, wrap the yarn around three times to create a triple yarn over.

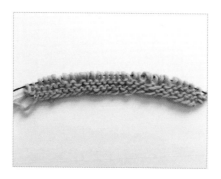

5 Knit a stitch, work a double yarn over again, knit one, single yarn over, then knit six. Repeat from * to the end of the row. You can see the needle crowded with extra yarn overs between stitches.

6 Turn your work to the right side, and on the next row start by knitting six stitches, which will take you to the first yarn over from the previous row.

7 Simply drop this stitch off the needle. Don't worry – it won't go anywhere!

8 Repeat with the double and triple yarn overs, knitting the stitches in between, until you come to the next knit section. You can see the pattern of elongated stitches emerging already. Carry on in the same way to the end of the row.

9 Knit two rows, ending with a wrong-side row.

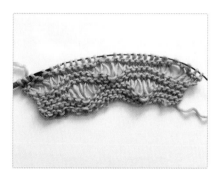

TOP TIP
Place stitch markers in between each lace pattern repeat on the borders to keep track of your knitting more easily.

10 In the next section, the elongated stitches will match up with the knitted parts of the last set of yarn overs and dropped stitches, so knit just one stitch before starting your pattern of single, double and triple yarn overs.

11 Here, after a couple more knit rows, you can see the wave-like pattern, which will show up even better once it has been gently blocked.

SEA FOAM SHAWLETTE

ELONGATED STITCHES CAN SEEM SOMEWHAT ALARMING TO WORK WITH, BUT DON'T WORRY – THIS SUPER-SOFT YARN IS STRONGER THAN IT LOOKS. THE PATTERN CREATED USING YARN OVERS AND THEN DROPPING THEM GIVES THIS SHAWLETTE A STRIKING WAVE-LIKE EFFECT, WHICH IS PERFECT FOR A LONG STROLL WATCHING THE BREAKERS ON THE BEACH.

ABOUT THIS YARN
Triskelion yarn is made by Caerthan Wrack, who kettle-dyes all his yarns by hand in Wales, in the UK, using single-pigment dyes to yield rich, strong colours with subtle details. Nimbus blends Suri alpaca with silk for a really luxurious knit, but if you want to try something different you could try knitting this shawlette in your favourite mohair and silk blend.

TECHNIQUES
Casting on – page 18
Knit stitch – page 20
Purl stitch – page 21
Yarn overs – page 38
Knit front and back – page 31
Decreasing – page 32
Elongated stitches – page 104
Casting off – page 22

SIZE
Long edge: 54in (137cm)
Depth at deepest point:
12¾in (32cm)

TENSION
21 sts and 26 rows to 4in (10cm) over st st.
Tension is not critical to this project.

YOU WILL NEED
Triskelion Nimbus 75% Suri alpaca, 25% silk (approx 328yd/300m per 50g)
1 x 50g hank in Emerald
4mm (UK8:US6) needles
Stitch markers

Note: Yarn amounts given are based on average requirements and are approximate.

ABBREVIATIONS
See page 148.

SEA FOAM WAVE PATTERN
Worked over a multiple of 10 sts + 6
Row 1 (RS): Knit.
Row 2: K6, *yo, k1, yo twice, k1, yo 3 times, k1, yo twice, k1, yo, k6*; rep from * to *.
Row 3: K6, **drop yo from previous row, k1, drop double yo from previous row, k1, drop triple yo from previous row, k1, drop double yo from previous row, k1, drop yo from previous row, k6**; rep from ** to **.
Rows 4 and 5: Knit.
Row 6: K1, rep from * to * as in row 2.
Row 7: K1, rep from ** to ** as in row 3.
Row 8: Knit.
These 8 rows form patt and are repeated.

SHAWLETTE
Cast on 5 sts.
Knit 1 row.
Row 1 (RS): K1, yo, ssk, kfb, yo, k1 (7 sts).
Row 2: K3, k2tog, k2 (6 sts).
Row 3: K1, yo, ssk, k1, kfb, yo, k1 (8 sts).
Row 4: K3, p1, k2tog, k2 (7 sts).
Row 5: K1, yo, ssk, k2, kfb, yo, k1 (9 sts).
Row 6: K3, p2, k2tog, k2 (8 sts).

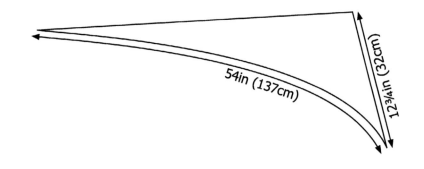

SET BOOMERANG PATTERN

Row 1 (RS): K1, yo, ssk, k to last 2 sts, kfb, k1.

Row 2: K3, p to last 4 sts, k2tog, k2.

These 2 rows set patt, with 1 st increased over each 2 rows.

Rep these 2 rows until you have 100 sts, ending with row 2.

Piece meas approx 33in (84cm) along the edge where decreases take place.

SET SEA FOAM WAVE STITCH

Row 1 (RS): K1, yo, ssk, k8, pm1, work row 1 of Sea Foam Wave Patt to last 3 sts, pm2, k1, kfb, yo, k1.

Row 2: K3, p to m, sm, work row 2 of Sea Foam Wave Patt to m, sm, p to last 4 sts, k2tog, k2.

Row 3: K1, yo, ssk, k to m, sm, work row 3 of Sea Foam Wave Patt to m, sm, k to last 2 sts, kfb, yo, k1.

Row 4: K3, p to m, sm, work row 4 of Sea Foam Wave Patt to m, sm, k to last 4 sts, k2tog, k2.

These 4 rows set position of Sea Foam Wave Patt. Cont as set until you have worked 2 full reps of patt, then move markers to include 1 patt rep fewer on the decrease side and 1 more on the increase side.

Work 2 more full reps of Sea Foam Wave Patt between markers, then remove markers.

SET GARTER STITCH BORDER

Row 1: K1, yo, ssk, k to last 2 sts, kfb, yo, k1.

Row 2: K to last 4 sts, k2tog, k2.

Rep these 2 rows until you have nearly run out of yarn or shawl reaches desired length, then cast off loosely kwise.

TO FINISH

Weave in ends (see page 71).
Block (see page 23).

BRIOCHE KNITTING

Brioche knitting is widely reputed to be challenging, but in fact it is one of the simplest and most pleasing techniques I've encountered. Using slipped stitches worked together on the next row, it creates a squashy, reversible ribbed fabric and a wonderful colour effect when worked in two shades. Brioche also has a lovely rhythm that is perfect for knitters who want their craft to be about relaxation and wellbeing.

ONE-COLOUR BRIOCHE

1 Brioche starts with a set-up row. The order of knitted and slipped stitches will vary from pattern to pattern; in this case, we will start with a simple knit stitch. *Bring the yarn to the front of the work.

2 Slip the next stitch purlwise, still holding the yarn at the front of the work.

3 Knit the next stitch as normal, creating a yarn over across the slipped stitch. Repeat from * to the end of the row, or as your pattern directs.

4 On the next row, you will see ordinary knit stitches alternating with slipped stitches with a yarn over. As you come to each knit stitch, bring the yarn to the front, then slip the stitch purlwise, as in step 2. This is known as slip one, yarn over (sl1yo).

5 The next stitch is a slipped stitch with a yarn over across it. Knit the slipped stitch together with its yarn over. This is called brioche knit 1, or brk1. It will also create a yarn over across the stitch you just slipped.

6 Continue to work in this way until you are directed otherwise by your pattern. Each row is worked in the same way, regardless of whether it is a RS or a WS row. The result is a reversible ribbed fabric.

TWO-COLOUR BRIOCHE

1 On a circular or double-pointed needle, work a set up row and a single row of (sl1yo, brk1) in colour A, just as you would in one-colour brioche. At the end of the row, do not turn the work. Slide the stitches back to the other end of the needle to work this side again.

2 Join B and purl the first stitch together with its yarn over. This is known as brioche purl 1, or brp1.

3 Slip the next stitch purlwise.

4 Take the yarn over the top of the needles to the back of the work, then back to the front of the work between the needles to create the yarn over across the slipped stitch.

5 The yarn is now at the front, ready to work the next brp stitch. Continue in this way to the end of the row, then turn the work.

6 On the next row use A to work a row of (brp1, sl1yo), as you did on the previous row with B. At the end of the row, do not turn the work but slide the stitches back to the other end to work that side again.

7 Now use B to work a row of (sl1yo, brk1). At the end of the row, turn the work.

8 These four rows form two-colour brioche and are repeated. The result is a reversible two-colour ribbed fabric with A dominant on one side...

9 ...and B dominant on the other side.

WRAPPED UP COWL

THIS VERSATILE WRAP IS SIMPLY A BIG, SOFT AND CUDDLY LOOP THAT YOU CAN WRAP ROUND AND
ROUND YOURSELF LIKE A GIANT SNOOD, OR CROSS OVER YOUR SHOULDERS TO FORM AN ELEGANT SHRUG.

ABOUT THIS YARN

Cascade Yarns, based near
Seattle, Washington, is a
family-run business that
aims to create high quality,
affordable yarns. Aereo is a
super-soft, blown blend of
baby alpaca, Merino wool
and a bit of nylon thrown in
for strength. As well as the
original range of solid and
heathered shades, it also
comes in a tweed version.

TECHNIQUES

Casting on – page 18
One-colour brioche – page 108
Casting off – page 22
Sewing up – page 70

SIZE

Width: 100in (254cm)
Depth: 21in (53cm)
After seaming: 21 x 50in (53 x 127cm)

TENSION

11 sts x 36 rows to 10cm over
brioche rib. *Use larger or smaller
needles if necessary to obtain
correct tension.*

YOU WILL NEED

Cascade Aereo 47% Merino wool,
31% baby alpaca, 22% nylon
(approx 240yd/220m per 100g)
6 x 100g skeins in 14 Lake Chelan
Heather
5.5mm (UK5:US9) needles

Note: Yarn amounts given are
based on average requirements
and are approximate.

ABBREVIATIONS

See page 148.

SPECIAL ABBREVIATIONS

brk1 = brioche knit 1: knit the next
stitch and the yarn over sitting over
the top of it together as one stitch
sl1yo = slip 1 yarn over: bring the yarn
to the front of the work, slip the next
st pwise, then knit the next st as
directed by the pattern, creating a
yarn over across the slipped stitch

PATTERN NOTE

Both sides are identical in this design
so there is no right or wrong side.

COWL

Cast on 64 sts.
Row 1: K1, (sl1yo, k1) to last st, k1.
Row 2: Sl1 kwise, (sl1yo, brk1) to last
st, k1.
Row 2 sets brioche rib patt.

Rep row 2 until piece meas 100in
(254cm).

Cast off as foll: Sl1 kwise, k1, *brk1,
pass first st on RH needle over
second, k1, pass first st on RH needle
over second; rep from * to end.
Fasten off last st.

TO FINISH

Sew cast-on to cast-off edge.
Weave in ends (see page 71).
Block gently if necessary (see
page 23).

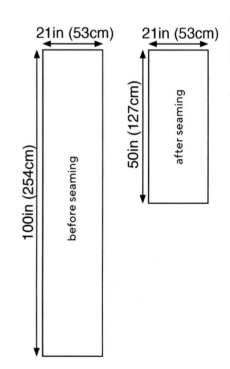

21in (53cm)   21in (53cm)

100in (254cm)   50in (127cm)

before seaming   after seaming

ELEMENTAL WRAP

EXPLORE THE BEAUTY OF ONE AND TWO-COLOUR BRIOCHE IN THIS SIMPLE GRADIENT WRAP. YOU'RE SURE TO BE LULLED BY THE GENTLE RHYTHM OF YOUR STITCHES AND THE SHEEPY SHADES THAT EMERGE.

ABOUT THIS YARN

Based in the remote Uist islands in the Outer Hebrides, Uist Wool spins the fleece of local sheep on reclaimed machinery to create unique, rustic yarns. This wrap is a taster menu of the brand's range of DK wools in a whole spectrum of natural sheep shades.

TECHNIQUES

Casting on – page 18
Knit stitch – page 20
Purl stitch – page 21
One-colour brioche – page 108
Two-colour brioche – page 109
Casting off – page 22

SIZE

Width: approx 72¾in (185cm)
Depth: 13¾in (35cm)

TENSION

17 sts and 42 rows to 10cm over brioche rib. *Tension is not critical to this project.*

YOU WILL NEED

Uist Wool Solas DK 100% Cheviot wool (approx 262yd/240m per 100g)
1 x 100g hank in Natural White (A)
Uist Wool Fras DK 100% Cheviot and Zwartbles wool
(approx 257yd/235m per 100g)
1 x 100g hank in Silver Grey (B)
Uist Wool Sìth DK 100% Cheviot and Hebridean wool
(approx 241yd/220m per 100g)
1 x 100g hank in Light Cool Grey Blend (C)
Uist Wool Tìr DK 100% Black Welsh Mountain wool
(approx 262yd/240m per 100g)
1 x 100g hank in Natural Brown (D)
4mm (UK8:US6) circular needle

Note: Yarn amounts are based on average requirements and are approximate.

ABBREVIATIONS

See page 148.

SPECIAL ABBREVIATIONS

brk1 = brioche knit 1: knit the next st tog with the yo from the previous row
brp1 = brioche purl 1: purl the next st tog with the yo from the previous row
sl1yo = on a knit/brk row: bring the yarn to the front, slip the next st pwise then work the following st as normal, creating a yarn over across

the slipped st; on a purl/brp row: wyif, slip the next st pwise, then take the yarn back over the needle and bring it back to the front in between the needles ready to work the next st, creating a yarn over across the slipped st

PATTERN NOTES

This wrap is completely reversible, but a right side and wrong side are referred to in the instructions to aid knitting. It may be helpful to place a locking marker on the RS for your reference once the two sides are established at the start of the first Section 2. When working to the end of your yarn, make sure you leave a long enough tail to weave in ends.

SECTION 1: ONE-COLOUR BRIOCHE

Row 1: K1, (brk1, sl1yo) to last 2 sts, brk1, k1.
Row 2: K1, (sl1yo, brk1) to last 2 sts, sl1yo, k1.
These two rows repeated form brioche rib.

SECTION 2: TWO-COLOUR BRIOCHE

Row 1 (RS): In first colour k1, (brk1, sl1yo) to last 2 sts, brk1, k1, do not turn, slide sts back to other end of needle to work this side again.

Row 2 (RS): In second colour k1, (sl1yo, brp1) to last 2 sts, sl1yo, k1, turn.
Row 3 (WS): In first colour k1, (brp1, sl1yo) to last 2 sts, brp1, k1, do not turn, slide sts back to other end of needle to work this side again.
Row 4 (WS): In second colour k1, (sl1yo, brk1) to last 2 sts, sl1yo, turn.
These four rows repeated form two-colour brioche rib.

WRAP

Using A cast on 61 sts.
Set-up row: (K1, sl1yo) to last st, k1.
SET BRIOCHE RIB
Work Section 1 until piece meas approx 14¼in (36cm) or until you have used around three-quarters of yarn A.
Join B and work Section 2 with A as first colour and B as second colour until piece meas approx 24in (61cm) or until you have used all of A, ending with row 4.
Cont in B only, work Section 1 until piece meas approx 31½in (80cm) or

until you have used around three-quarters of B, ending with row 2.
Join C and work Section 2 with B as first colour and C as second colour until piece meas approx 41¼in (105cm) or until you have used all of B, ending with row 4.
Cont in C only, work Section 1 until piece meas approx 48¾in (124cm) or until you have used around three-quarters of C, ending with row 2.
Join D and work Section 2 with C as first colour and D as second colour until piece meas approx 58¾in (149cm) or until you have used all of C, ending with row 4.

Cont in D only, work Section 1 until piece meas approx 72¾in (185cm) or until you have used nearly all of D, ending on a WS row.
Cast off as foll on RS: K1, *brk1, pass first st on RH needle over second, p1, pass first st on RH needle over second; rep from * to last 2 sts, brk1, pass first st on RH needle over second, cast off final st as normal.

TO FINISH

Weave ends into the correct colour section as neatly as possible (see page 71).
Block if required (see page 23).

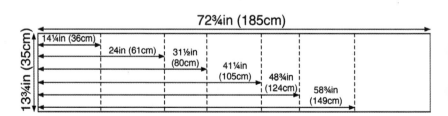

SHADES OF GREY SHAWL

THIS SIMPLE, CLASSIC TRIANGLE SHAWL SHOWS OFF SHADES OF GREY AND WHITE WOOL, AND IS ADORNED WITH A SIMPLE LACE SECTION WITH A LOVELY RHYTHMIC PATTERN THAT IS GREAT TO USE AS A MEDITATION.

ABOUT THIS YARN

Created by pioneering knitwear designer Erika Knight, Wool Local is sourced, scoured, combed, spun, dyed, steamed and hanked all in the county of Yorkshire in the north of England. A blend of luxurious Bluefaced Leicester and hardwearing Masham wool, it is a truly local fibre made in the heartland of Britain's historic textile industry.

TECHNIQUES

Casting on – page 18
Garter tab cast on – page 50
Knit stitch – page 20
Purl stitch – page 21
Yarn overs – page 38
Decreasing – page 32
Casting off – page 22

SIZE

Width before blocking: 73¼in (186cm)
Width after blocking: 75in (190cm)
Depth before blocking: 36½in (93cm)
Depth after blocking: 37in (95cm)

TENSION

26 sts and 30 rows to 10cm over st st before blocking. *Tension is not critical to this project.*

YOU WILL NEED

Erika Knight Wool Local
100% British wool (approx 492yd/450m per 100g)
Alternative yarn suggestions: This design would work well for any 4 ply or fingering-weight yarn, such as Jamieson & Smith Shetland Heritage, John Arbon Exmoor Sock or Cascade 220 Fingering.
1 x 100g hank in Fairfax (A)
1 x 100g hank in Gritstone (B)
1 x 100g hank in Ted (C)
3.5mm (UK9:US4) needles
6 stitch markers

Note: Yarn amounts are based on average requirements and are approximate.

ABBREVIATIONS

See page 148.

LACE PATTERN

Worked over 4 sts
Row 1 (RS): K2, yo, ssk.
Row 2: Purl.
Row 3: K2, k2tog, yo.
Row 4: Purl.
These 4 rows form pattern and are repeated.

STRIPE SEQUENCE

2 rows A
2 rows B
2 rows C

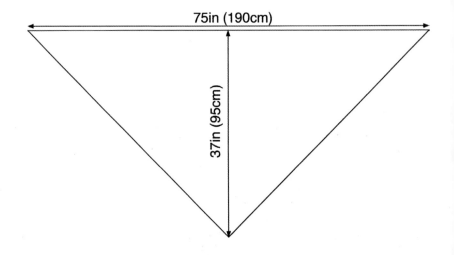

75in (190cm)

37in (95cm)

SHAWL

Using A, cast on 6 sts.

SET LACE TAB

Row 1: Work row 1 of Lace Patt, k2.

Row 2: Purl.

These 2 rows set position of Lace Patt and st st. Cont as set until you have worked 3 full reps of 4-row Lace Patt, then knit 1 RS row.

Do not turn work but, with RS facing, rotate piece 90 degrees and pick up 6 sts along side edge, rotate 90 degrees again and pick up 6 sts from cast-on edge (18 sts).
Purl 1 row.

SET SHAWL SHAPING AND STRIPE SEQUENCE

Set-up row: Using A, *work Lace Patt over 4 sts, k2, pm, yo, pm; rep from * once more, work Lace Patt over next 4 sts, k2 (20 sts).

Next row: Purl.

Row 1: Using B, *work 4 sts in Lace Patt, k2, sm, yo, k to m, yo, sm; rep from * once more, work 4 sts in Lace Patt, k2 (inc 4).

Row 2: Purl.

Rows 1 and 2 set patt. Cont in patt as set, working in six-row stripe sequence and repeating rows 1 and 2 until you have worked a total of 182 rows, ending with 2 rows in A (380 sts).
Piece meas approx 30in (76cm).

SET LACE SECTION

Break A and C and cont in B only.

Row 1 (RS): Patt 6 as set, sm, yo, pm, work the same row of Lace Patt as for border to last st before m, pm, k1, yo, sm, patt 6 as set, sm, yo, pm, work in Lace Patt as before to last st before m, pm, k1, yo, sm, patt as set to end.

Row 2: Purl.

Row 3: Patt 6, sm, yo, k to m, sm, patt as set to m, sm, k to m, yo, sm, patt 6, sm, yo, k to m, sm, patt as set to m, sm, k to m, yo, sm, patt to end.

Row 4: Purl.

Rows 3 and 4 set patt. Cont in patt as now set. Each time you have 4 more sts between the border and pattern markers or the pattern and spine markers, move marker and work one more pattern repeat, always working the pattern row you have been working throughout.

Cont as set in B only until you have worked a total of 36 rows in lace patt (452 sts).

SET EDGE PATT

Cont in lace patt as set, but work in stripes as foll:

2 rows C

2 rows A

2 rows B (464 sts).

Using C, work rows 1 and 2 of first section, with st st in between lace borders (468 sts).

I-CORD CAST OFF

Using C, cast off as foll: *K2, k2tog, slip sts from RH needle back to LH needle; rep from * until 3 sts rem, k3tog, fasten off.

TO FINISH

Weave in ends (see page 71).
Block firmly to open out lace (see page 23).

SLIP STITCH COLOURWORK

Slipping stitches is a great way to add colour to your knitting without using more than one yarn on a single row or round. Here's how to work linen stitch for the Harvest Home Cowl on page 122. Remember to always slip stitches purlwise, so they are not twisted when you come to work them.

1 Starting with colour A, knit one stitch.

2 Bring the yarn to the front.

3 Slip the next stitch purlwise.

4 Take the yarn to the back of the work, ready to knit the next stitch. Repeat from step 1 to the end of the round.

TOP TIP
Slip stitch patterns can end up as quite tight, dense fabric. If the fabric is coming out firmer than you want, try out a larger needle size.

5 On the next round, still using A, slip the first stitch purlwise with the yarn at the front, then knit the second stitch. Repeat these two stitches to the end of the round. Once your first pattern repeat is complete the slipped stitches will be in one shade and the knitted stitches in the other.

6 Now pick up yarn B. Working as for round 1, knit one stitch, then slip the second stitch purlwise with the yarn at the front. Repeat to the end of the round.

7 On the following round, work as in step 5, but still using colour B.

8 Repeat these four rounds, swapping between A and B, to build up a pretty pattern that has almost a woven effect.

HARVEST HOME COWL

ORGANICALLY FARMED MERINO FROM THE FALKLAND ISLANDS MEETS DEVON ZWARTBLES WOOL IN THIS LOVELY WORSTED-WEIGHT WOOL FROM SPINNER JOHN ARBON, WHO IS BASED IN DEVON, SOUTHWEST ENGLAND. THIS SIMPLE COWL IS KNITTED IN THE ROUND FROM JUST TWO SKEINS OF YARN AND INTRODUCES THE COLOUR MARVEL THAT IS LINEN STITCH.

ABOUT THIS YARN

Harvest Hues is one of Devon spinner John Arbon's most popular yarns in a 4 ply version, and this plumper, worsted or light aran-weight alternative is perfect for quick knits and cooler weather. Devon-grown Zwartbles fleece is naturally dark and is blended with pre-dyed Merino shades to give a palette of deeply complex, heathered shades.

TECHNIQUES

Casting on – page 18
Jogless join – page 27
Knitting in the round – page 26
Knit stitch – page 20
Purl stitch – page 21
Slip stitch colourwork – page 120
Casting off – page 22

SIZE

Circumference: 22in (56cm)
Depth: 7in (18cm)

TENSION

23 sts and 25 rnds to 4in (10cm) over g st using 4mm needle.
23 sts and 45 rnds to 4in (10cm) over linen st using 5.5mm needle.
Use larger or smaller needles if necessary to obtain correct tension.

YOU WILL NEED

John Arbon Harvest Hues Worsted
65% organically farmed Falklands Merino wool, 35% Devon Zwartbles wool (approx 219yd/200m per 100g)
1 x 100g hank in Barley (A)
1 x 100g hank in Woad (B)
4mm (UK8:US6) and 5.5mm (UK5:US9) circular needles
Stitch marker

Note: Yarn amounts are based on average requirements and are approximate.

ABBREVIATIONS

See page 148.

PATTERN NOTE

Slip stitches purlwise.

COWL

Using 4mm needles and A cast on 131 sts. Join to work in the round, taking care not to twist sts, and

pm to mark beg of rnd.
**Knit 1 rnd.
Purl 1 rnd.
Rep last 2 rnds once more, then knit 1 more rnd.**

SET LINEN STITCH

Change to 5.5mm needles.
Rnd 1: Using A, (k1, sl1 wyif) to last st, k1.
Rnd 2: Using A, (sl1 wyif, k1) to last st, sl1 wyif.
Rnds 3 and 4: As rnds 1 and 2 but using B.
Rep rnds 1–4 thirteen more times.
Break B and cont in A only.
Rep rnds 1 and 2 once more.
Change to 4mm needles.
Rep from ** to ** once more.
Cast off loosely.

TO FINISH

Weave in ends (see page 71).
Block (see page 23).

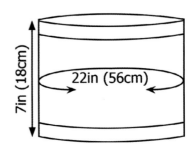

BEYOND BASICS

ADORN YOUR SHAWLS WITH ADVANCED TECHNIQUES

*'It's much easier than I thought it would be.
Most things in knitting are, really.'*

GILL MCNEIL, THE BEACH STREET KNITTING
SOCIETY AND YARN CLUB

SHOPAHOLICS

How and where to find yarn!

I love shopping. I love shopping more than I love actually owning stuff, so I try to keep it to windows and browsing as much as I can. I don't really need any more yarn, probably ever – I have reached the state of SABLE, which means that my yarn Stash Acquisition has gone Beyond my Life Expectancy. But from time to time there is a really good excuse for buying more yarn. Or maybe you are just starting out on building your stash. So where will you buy it?

It gives me great pleasure to support small, innovative businesses and especially inspiring independent retailers, so the first place I look for in any new town is a local independent yarn shop. Many of these businesses go far beyond simply selling yarn – as well as all the needles, notions and gorgeous project bags you could imagine they offer classes, free advice on knitting problems, help choosing patterns and much, much more.

The Covid-19 pandemic lockdowns of 2020 and 2021 forced many of these businesses to think differently about how they operated, and retailers introduced all sorts of new services, which have meant that they can now sell far beyond their own doorsteps. Some invited customers to one-on-one virtual personal shopping sessions, where they could be taken around the shop on a video link and get advice on what to buy as they browsed. Others took to Instagram to open their shops up live on social media, and moved regular knitting groups online so they didn't lose touch with regular customers. If you've ever fallen in love with a yarn shop on holiday, why not see if you can pay it a virtual visit from the comfort of your own home?

ALL THE FUN OF THE FAIR

However, nothing beats actually handling and squishing yarn before you buy. We knitters tend to be tactile people, so where it is possible and safe to do so, we'd love to see our yarn in

person before we invest. A great way to see lots of yarn all in one place, and to meet the people who actually make it, is to visit a yarn or fibre festival. These exciting events take place all over the world, and range from small fairs run by local knitting and crochet guilds to massive events, such as the Edinburgh Yarn Festival and Yarndale in the UK, and the New York State Sheep and Wool Festival in Rhinebeck, New York, which welcome visitors from all over the globe. In 2020, lockdown restrictions encouraged many of these shows' organisers to launch virtual events, making them accessible to those who, for whatever reason, couldn't attend in person, and which look set to continue well beyond the pandemic.

ON HOME TURF

One of the great things about meeting producers in person is to hear stories of where your yarn comes from, the inspiration behind it and the maker's take on what sort of designs it works best with. But you can go a step further and even visit some producers on their home turf. Some of the spinners featured in this book offer mill visits, either on open days, by special appointment or as part of a tourism drive in their area. Why not research the suppliers section on page 150 and see if any of the producers in this book are somewhere near you, or near your next holiday destination?

Of course, there are many other ways of finding yarn, and online retailers such as LoveCrafts, Wool Warehouse, WEBS and Jimmy Beans Wool sell huge ranges at the click of a button, and often offer very competitive deals. It's a yarny world out there, so delve in and see what you can find.

FIND YOUR YARN

- Google local yarn shops.
- Pick a favourite yarn brand and see if it has a store locator.
- Find UK yarn shops at ukhandknitting.com.
- Find yarn shops worldwide at knitmap.com – but Google the stores before visiting, as this site is not completely up to date.
- Look up your favourite yarn brand and see if you can visit its mill.

CUDDLE WRAP

THIS SWEET WRAP BLANKET INTRODUCES AN ALL-OVER LACE CHEVRON PATTERN WITH A LOVELY RHYTHM TO THE REPEATED STITCHES. IT MAKES A GREAT GIFT FOR A BABY AND A NEW PARENT.

ABOUT THIS YARN

Designer Debbie Bliss made a name for herself knitting cacti during the punk days of the 1980s before launching her own yarn brand. Machine-washable, tumble-dryable Cashmerino Aran comes in a wide range of colours and meets all the criteria for a great baby knit.

TECHNIQUES

Casting on – page 18
Knit stitch – page 20
Purl stitch – page 21
Yarn overs – page 38
Decreasing – page 32
Casting off – page 22

SIZE

Width: 56¼in (143cm)
Depth: 22in (56cm)

TENSION

17 sts and 19 rows to 4in (10cm) over pattern. *Use larger or smaller needles if necessary to obtain correct tension.*

YOU WILL NEED

Debbie Bliss Cashmerino Aran
55% extrafine Merino wool, 33% acrylic, 12% cashmere (approx 98yd/90m per 50g)
3 x 50g balls in 25 White (A)
3 x 50g balls in 09 Grey (B)
2 x 50g balls in 603 Baby Pink (C)
2 x 50g balls in 46 Heather (D)
5mm (UK6:US8) needles

Note: Yarn amounts given are based on average requirements and are approximate.

ABBREVIATIONS

See page 148.

STRIPE SEQUENCE

**4 rows A
2 rows B
2 rows A
4 rows B
4 rows C
2 rows D
2 rows C
4 rows D
4 rows B
2 rows A
2 rows B
4 rows A**
4 rows D
2 rows C
2 rows D
4 rows C
·These 48 rows form Stripe Sequence.

COLOUR STRIPE SEQUENCE

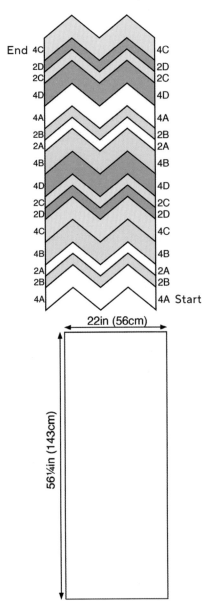

End	4C		4C
	2D		2D
	2C		2C
	4D		4D
	4A		4A
	2B		2B
	2A		2A
	4B		4B
	4D		4D
	2C		2C
	2D		2D
	4C		4C
	4B		4B
	2A		2A
	2B		2B
	4A		4A Start

22in (56cm)

56¼in (143cm)

WRAP

Using A, cast on 96 sts.
Knit 2 rows.

SET CHEVRON PATTERN AND STRIPE SEQUENCE

Working in Stripe Sequence, set chevron patt as foll:

Row 1 (RS): K2, (k1, yo, k4, k2tog, ssk, k4, yo) 7 times to last 3 sts, k3.

Row 2: K3, p to last 3 sts, k3.

These 2 rows set chevron patt.

Rep these 2 rows, working Stripe Sequence 5 times, then working Stripe Sequence from ** to ** once more.

Cont in A only, knit 2 rows.

Cast off.

TO FINISH

Weave in ends (see page 71).
Block firmly (see page 23) to open out pattern. Use pins to accentuate points.

HAP-PINESS HAP

THIS DESIGN IS BASED ON A TRADITIONAL SHETLAND HAP SHAWL. IT STARTS WITH A GARTER STITCH SQUARE KNITTED BACK AND FORTH, ON THE BIAS. ONCE THIS SQUARE IS COMPLETE, STITCHES ARE PICKED UP AROUND ALL FOUR SIDES AND THE BORDER IS KNITTED IN THE ROUND, IN A TRADITIONAL SHETLAND STITCH PATTERN.

ABOUT THIS YARN

Knitter Rachel Atkinson founded Daughter of a Shepherd in a bid to save her shepherd father's fleece from being wasted. Her Ram Jam yarn combines fleece from all sorts of beautiful British sheep breeds.

TECHNIQUES

Slipknot – page 17
Knit stitch – page 20
Purl stitch – page 21
Yarn overs – page 38
Increasing – page 30
Decreasing – page 32
Stitch markers – page 47
Casting off – page 22

SIZE

Whole hap unblocked: 33½in (85cm) square
Whole hap blocked: 40in (101.5cm) square
Centre square unblocked: 14½in (37cm) square
Centre square blocked: 17¾in (45cm) square

TENSION

18 sts and 36 rows to 4in (10cm) over Centre Square garter stitch and eyelet pattern after blocking.
Use larger or smaller needles if necessary to obtain correct tension.

YOU WILL NEED

Daughter of a Shepherd Ram Jam Sport 100% British wool from mixed breeds
(approx 126yd/115m per 50g)
Sample knitted in wool from the 2018 clip
1 x 50g skein in 1.5 In-between Grey (A)
1 x 50g skein in 0 Natural White (B)
1 x 50g skein in 1 Light Grey (C)
1 x 50g skein in 2 Mid Grey (D)
1 x 50g skein in 3 Natural Black (E)
4mm (UK8:US6) needles
2-4 x 4mm (UK8:US 6) long circular needles
Stitch markers

Note: Yarn amounts given are based on average requirements and are approximate.

ABBREVIATIONS

See page 148.

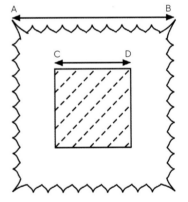

A to B: 33½in (85cm) unblocked
40in (101.5cm) blocked

C to D: 14½in (37cm) unblocked
17¾in (45cm) blocked

CHART

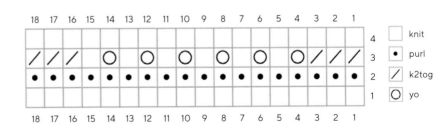

18	17	16	15	14	13	12	11	10	9	8	7	6	5	4	3	2	1		4
	/	/	/		O		O		O		O		O		O	/	/	/	3
	•	•	•	•	•	•	•	•	•	•	•	•	•	•	•	•	•	•	2
																			1
18	17	16	15	14	13	12	11	10	9	8	7	6	5	4	3	2	1		

KEY

☐	knit
•	purl
/	k2tog
O	yo

OLD SHALE STITCH
Worked over 18 sts
Rnd 1: Knit.
Rnd 2: Purl.
Rnd 3: (K2tog) 3 times, (yo, k1)
6 times, (k2tog) 3 times.
Rnd 4: Knit.

HAP
CENTRE SQUARE
Using A and 4mm needles,
make a slip knot.
Row 1: Kyok (3 sts).
Row 2: Knit.
Row 3: K1, m1L, k1, m1R, k1 (5 sts).
Row 4: Knit.
SET INCREASE PATT
Row 1 (RS): K1, m1L, k to last st, m1R,
k1 (7 sts).
Row 2: Knit.

Rep rows 1 and 2 eleven more times
(29 sts).
Eyelet inc row 1 (RS): K1, yo, (k2tog,
yo) to last 2 sts, k1, yo, k1 (31 sts).
Eyelet inc row 2: Knit.
*Rep rows 1 and 2 eight more times
(47 sts).
Rep eyelet inc rows 1 and 2 once more
(49 sts).
Rep from * 3 more times (103 sts).
SET DECREASE PATT
***Row 1 (RS):** K1, ssk, k to last 3 sts,
k2tog, k1 (dec 2).
Row 2: Knit.
Rep rows 1 and 2 seven more times
(87 sts).
Eyelet dec row 1: K1, ssk, (yo, k2tog)
to last 4 sts, yo, k3tog, k1 (85 sts).
Eyelet dec row 2: Knit.
Rep from * 3 more times (31 sts).

Then rep rows 1 and 2 until 7 sts rem.
Next row: K1, ssk, k1, k2tog, k1 (5 sts).
Next row: Knit.
Next row: K1, k3tog, k1 (3 sts).
Next row: Knit.
Next row: K3tog, fasten off.
BORDER SET-UP
Using B and long circular needle,
with RS facing, *pick up and knit 1 st
in corner, yo, pm, pick up and knit
90 sts along one side of square, pm,
yo, pm; rep from * on rem 3 corners
and sides of square (372 sts: 1 at each
corner with a yarn over on each side
counting as 1 st each, and 90 sts
along each side of the square).
Next rnd: *K1, yo, (k to m, sm) twice,
k to m, yo, sm; rep from * 3 more times
(380 sts).

SET OLD SHALE PATT AND
CORNER INCREASES
Rnd 1: *K1, yo, k to m, sm, work row 1
of Old Shale Patt to m, sm, k to m, yo,
sm; rep from * 3 times (inc 8).
Rnd 2: *K1, yo, p to m, sm, work row 2
of Old Shale Patt to m, sm, p to m, yo,
sm; rep from * 3 times (inc 8).
Rnd 3: *K1, yo, k to m, sm, work row 3
of Old Shale Patt to m, sm, k to m, yo,
sm; rep from * 3 times (inc 8).
Rnd 4: *K1, yo, k to m, sm, work row 4
of Old Shale Patt to m, sm, k to m,
yo, sm; rep from * 3 times (inc 8).
These 4 rnds set pattern. Cont in patt,
working in stripe patt as foll:
4 rnds in D
4 rnds in C
4 rnds in E
You should now have 508 sts: 1 at
each corner and 126 along each side.
There are now 18 sts between each
corner stitch and the stitch marker at
the start of the Old Shale pattern.
Break E and cont in B.
****Next rnd:** *K1, yo, pm, work row 1
of Old Shale patt over next 18 sts,

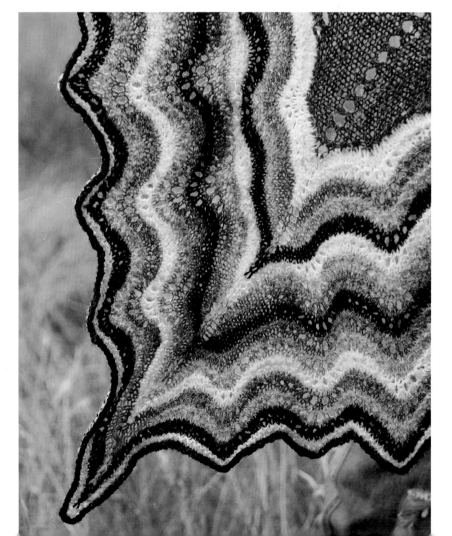

remove marker, work row 1 of Old Shale patt to next m, remove marker, work row 1 of Old Shale patt over next 18 sts, pm, yo, sm; rep from * 3 times (inc 8).**

This rnd sets new position of Old Shale patt. Cont as set above, working rnds 2–4 in B as set, then cont working rnds 1–4 in stripe patt as foll:

4 rnds C

4 rnds D

4 rnds E

4 rnds D

668 sts: 1 at each corner and 166 on each side.

Break D and cont in C.

Next rnd: *K1, yo, k2, pm, work row 1 of Old Shale patt over next 18 sts, remove marker, work row 1 of Old Shale Patt to next m, remove marker, work row 1 of Old Shale patt over next 18 sts, pm, k2, yo, sm; rep from * 3 times (inc 8).

This rnd sets new position of Old Shale patt. Cont as set above, working rnds 2–4 in C as set, then cont working rnds 1–4 in stripe patt as foll:

4 rnds B

4 rnds in D

4 rnds in C

796 sts: 1 at each corner and 198 on each side

Change to E and work from ** to ** (804 sts).

This rnd sets new position of Old Shale patt. Cont as set, working rnds 2–4 in E as set (828 sts).

Change to B and work rnds 1 and 2 of Old Shale patt (844 sts).

Change to E and work rnds 1 and 2 of Old Shale patt (860 sts).

Using E, cast off loosely pwise.

TO FINISH

Weave in ends (see page 71).

Block firmly to open out stitch pattern (see page 23).

TRUE COLOURS SHAWLETTE

THERE'S NOTHING AS SATISFYING AS CREATING YOUR OWN TOTALLY UNIQUE YARN AND THEN KNITTING IT INTO SOMETHING BEAUTIFUL. EXCEPT PERHAPS FOR KNITTING SOMETHING BEAUTIFUL FROM A SKEIN OF YARN SOMEONE ELSE HAS DYED. THIS LITTLE SHAWLETTE IS KNITTED IN A STANDARD 4 PLY YARN, SO IF YOU DON'T FANCY DYEING YOURSELF, SIMPLY SWAP FOR A PRE-DYED WOOL.

ABOUT THIS YARN

It's a Stitch Up's Suzie Blackman sources yarns ethically and hand-dyes them in her studio in East London – but she also gives knitters the tools to create their own amazing colours with her dye kits. This project started out as a hand-dyeing kit and evolved into this unique knit.

TECHNIQUES

Casting on – page 18
Knit stitch – page 20
Purl stitch – page 21
Yarn overs – page 38
Decreasing – page 32
Stitch markers – page 47
Casting off – page 22

SIZE

Width: 71¼in (181cm)
Depth: 13in (33cm)

TENSION

23 sts x 33 rows to 4in (10cm) over g st.
Use larger or smaller needles if necessary to obtain correct tension.

YOU WILL NEED

It's A Stitch Up Yarn Dyeing Kit with turquoise and magenta dyes 100% superwash Merino 4 ply (approx 400yd/365m per 100g) 1 x 100g hank OR 365m of any 4 ply yarn in the shade of your choice
4mm (UK8:US6) needles
2 stitch markers

Note: Yarn amounts are based on average requirements and are approximate.

PATTERN NOTES

To create your own totally unique shawlette, use the kit to dye your own speckled yarn before you cast on. If dyeing's not your thing, just pick any 4 ply yarn – the sample was knitted in superwash Merino. This shawlette is knitted from side to side like a scarf.

ABBREVIATIONS

See page 148.

SPECIAL ABBREVIATIONS

ssp = slip slip purl: slip 2 sts kwise, then slip them back to LH needle and ptog tbl

TOP TIP

Separate your different stitch patterns with stitch markers as indicated in the text. If you have any trouble keeping track of where you are in the pattern, you may want to write out the instructions for each row and tick them off as you go along.

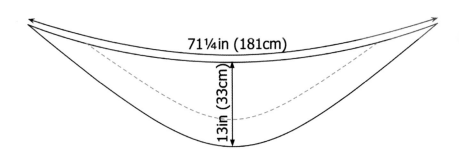

LACE ZIGZAG

Worked over 6 sts initially, increasing to 8 over pattern

Row 1: K1, p1, (yo, k1, p1) twice.

Rows 2, 4, 6, 8 and 10: (K1, p2tog, yo) twice, k1, p1.

Rows 3, 5, 7 and 9: K1, p1, (yo, k2tog, p1) twice.

Rows 11, 13, 15, 17 and 19: K1, p1, (ssk, yo, p1) twice.

Rows 12, 14, 16, 18 and 20: (K1, yo, slip kwise the yo from previous row and the next st then place them both back on LH needle and ptog) twice, k1, p1.

Row 21: K1, p1, (yo, ssk, p1) twice.

Rows 2–21 form patt and are repeated.

SHELL STITCH

Worked over 11 sts.

Row 1: K2, yo, ssk, k5, yo, k2tog.

Row 2 and all alt rows: Purl.

Row 3: K2, yo, k1, ssk, k4, yo, k2tog.

Row 5: K2, yo, k2, ssk, k3, yo, k2tog.

Row 7: K2, yo, k3, ssk, k2, yo, k2tog.

Row 9: K2, yo, k4, ssk, k1, yo, k2tog.

Row 11: K2, yo, k5, ssk, yo, k2tog.

Row 12: Purl.

These 12 rows form patt and are repeated.

SHAWLETTE

Cast on 4 sts.

Row 1 (RS): K2, yo, k1, p1 (5 sts).

Rows 2 and 4: K1, p1, k3.

Row 3: K2, p1, k1, p1.

Row 5: K2, yo, p1, k1, p1 (6 sts).

Rows 6 and 8: (K1, p1) twice, k2.

Row 7: K2, (k1, p1) twice.

Row 9: K2, yo, (k1, p1) twice (7 sts).

Rows 10 and 12: (K1, p1) twice, k3.

Row 11: K2, p1, (k1, p1) twice.

Row 13: K2, yo, p1, (k1, p1) twice (8 sts).

Row 14: (K1, p1) 3 times.

Row 15: K2, (k1, p1) 3 times.

Row 16: (K1, p1) 3 times.

SET ZIGZAG LACE

Row 1: K2, yo, pm1, work Zigzag Lace row 1 to end.

Row 2: Work Zigzag Lace row 2 to m, sm, p1, k2.

Row 3: K to m, sm, work Zigzag Lace row 3 to end.

Row 4: Work Zigzag Lace row 4 to m, sm, p1, k2.

Row 5: K to m, yo, sm, work Zigzag Lace patt to end.

Row 6: Work Zigzag Lace pattern to m, sm, p to last 2 sts, k2.

Row 7: K to m, sm, work Zigzag Lace patt to end.

Row 8: Work Zigzag Lace pattern to m, sm, p to last 2 sts, k2.

This section sets Zigzag Lace patt and increases. Cont in patt as set, repeating rows 5–8 until you have 21 sts.

SET SHELL STITCH

Row 1: K2, pm2, work row 1 of Shell St patt to m1, sm, work Zigzag Lace patt to end.

Rows 2 and 4: Work Zigzag Lace patt to m1, sm, work Shell St patt to m2, sm, k to end.

Row 3: K to m2, yo, sm, work Shell St patt to m1, sm, work Zigzag Lace patt to end (inc 1).

Row 5: K to m2, sm, work Shell St patt to m1, sm, work Zigzag Lace patt to end..

Row 6: Work Zigzag Lace patt to m1, sm, work Shell St patt to m2, sm, k to end.

This section sets Shell St patt and increases. Cont in patt as set, repeating rows 3–6 until piece meas approx 30½in (90.5cm), ending with Zigzag Lace patt row 20.

SET DECREASE PATT

Row 1 (RS): K to m2, sm, work Shell St patt to m1, sm, work Zigzag Lace patt to end.

Row 2: Work Zigzag Lace patt to m2, sm, work Shell St patt to m1, sm, k to end.

Row 3: K to 2 sts before m2, k2tog, yo, patt to end as set.

Row 4: Patt to m2 as set, k1, ssk, k to end (dec 1).

Rep these 4 rows until 3 sts rem in g st section (22 sts in total including yarn overs in Zigzag Lace patt). Remove m2 and cont as foll:

Row 1: K to m1, sm, patt to end.

Row 2: Patt to m1, sm, p to last 2 sts, k2.

Row 3: K to 2 sts before m1, k2tog, yo, sm, patt to end.

Row 4: Patt to m1, sm, p1, ssp, p to last 2 sts, k2 (dec 1).

Rep these 4 rows until 4 sts rem outside Zigzag Lace patt (12 sts in total including yarn overs in Zigzag Lace patt).

Next row (RS): K to m, remove m, k1, p1, (k2tog, p1) twice (10 sts).

Next row: (K1, p1) 3 times, p to last 2 sts, k2.

SET FINAL DECREASE PATT

Row 1: K2, k2tog, work each st as it appears – so k the k sts and p the p sts – to end (dec 1).

Rows 2–4: Work each st as it appears. Rep these 4 rows until 5 sts rem. Cast off.

TO FINISH

Weave in ends (see page 71). Block firmly to open out lace patterns (see page 23), using pins to accentuate points of Zigzag Lace.

BRIOCHE INCREASES AND DECREASES

Because brioche stitches work with ribs in pairs of two stitches, increasing and decreasing is a little more challenging than with plain knitting.

TWO-STITCH INCREASE (BRKYOBRK)

1 Brioche knit the next stitch and its yarn over, but don't slip the stitches off the needle.

2 Bring the yarn forward...

3 ... then brioche knit 1 again into the same stitches, creating a yarn over between the 2 brk stitches.

4 Slip the original stitches off the LH needle – you have increased two stitches, or one set of brioche ribs.

TOP TIP
Brioche increases in themselves are pretty straightforward – it's on the next row that things can get confusing, when you are changing from working brioche stitches to simple stitches. Make sure you keep track of all your stitches: if you're having trouble it may be worth placing a marker at the increased stitch so you know when you come to it on the next row.

FOUR-STITCH INCREASE (BR4STINC)

1 Brioche knit the next stitch and its yarn over but don't slip the stitch off the needle.

2 Bring the yarn forward…

3 …brioche knit the same stitch and yarn over again…

4 …bring the yarn forward again…

5 …and brioche knit the same stitch and its yarn over one more time.

6 Now slip the original stitch and yarn over off the needle. You have increased four stitches, or two brioche ribs.

LEFT-SLANTING TWO-STITCH DECREASE (BRLSL DEC)

1 Start with sl1yo as usual.

2 Slip the next stitch and its yarn over kwise.

3 Brioche knit the following two stitches (one single stitch and one plus its yarn over) together.

4 Pass the slipped stitches over.

5 You have decreased two stitches and you can see the lean to the left.

TOP TIP
With all these steps brioche decreases can look pretty daunting – but don't worry, after you've worked a few they'll soon become second nature. They also show up very clearly in the knitting, which helps you to see when to work the next one.

RIGHT-SLANTING TWO-STITCH DECREASE: (BRRSL DEC)

1 Slip the next stitch and its yarn over kwise.

2 Knit the next stitch.

3 Pass the slipped stitches over.

4 Slip the stitch created back to the left-hand needle.

5 Pass the following stitch and its yarn over over.

6 Slip the stitch back to RH needle.

7 You have decreased two stitches and can see the lean to the right.

FALLING LEAVES SHAWL

TWO-COLOUR BRIOCHE CREATES A STRIKING CONTRAST RIB. ADDING LACE AND SHAPING CAN MAKE STUNNING LEAFY PATTERNS, SHOWING OFF THE GORGEOUS PASTEL AUTUMN SHADES OF THIS HAND-DYED YARN.

ABOUT THIS YARN

Vykky MacIntosh has been creating with yarn since she was just seven years old. She hand-dyes her yarns in her studio in West Sussex, UK, and takes the inspiration for her shades from 18th- and 19th-century literature.

TECHNIQUES

Casting on – page 18
Two-colour brioche – page 109
Brioche increases and decreases – page 138
Yarn overs – page 38
Casting off – page 22

SIZE

Width: 56in (142cm)
Depth: 35in (81cm)

TENSION

18 sts x 52 rows to 4in (10cm) over two-colour brioche rib. *Use larger or smaller needles if necessary to obtain correct tension.*

YOU WILL NEED

West Green Loft Yarns Cashmere Sock 80% Merino, 10% cashmere, 10% nylon (approx 383yd/350m per 100g)
1 x 100g skein in Maple (A)
1 x 100g skein in Regency (B)
3.5mm (UK9:US4) circular needle
Stitch markers

Note: Yarn amounts are based on average requirements and are approximate.

ABBREVIATIONS

See page 148.

SPECIAL ABBREVIATIONS

brk1 = brioche knit 1: knit the next stitch together with its yarn over
brp1 = brioche purl 1: purl the next stitch together with its yarn over
sl1yo = slip 1 yarn over: before a k or brk stitch, bring the working yarn forward, slip the next stitch pwise to the RH needle, then k or brk the following st, creating a yarn over across the slipped stitch; before a p or brp stitch, bring the yarn forward, slip the next st pwise to the RH needle, take the working yarn back over the needle then bring it forward in between the needle tips, creating a yarn over across the slipped st

brkyobrk = brioche knit the next stitch and its yarn over but don't slip the stitches off the needle, bring the yarn forward then brioche knit 1 again into the same stitches, creating a yarn over between the 2 brk stitches, then slip the original stitches off the LH needle (inc 2)
br4stinc = *brioche knit the next stitch and its yarn over but don't slip the stitch off the needle, yarn over; repeat from * once more, brioche knit 1 and slip the original stitch off the LH needle (inc 4)
brLsl dec = slip the next stitch and its yarn over kwise, brioche knit the following two stitches (one single stitch and one plus its yarn over) together, then pass the slipped stitches over (dec 2)
brRsl dec = slip the next stitch and its yarn over kwise, k the next stitch, pass the slipped stitches over, slip the stitch created back to the LH needle and pass the following stitch and its yarn over over, then slip stitch back to RH needle (dec 2)

BRIOCHE LACE PATTERN
Worked over 22 sts and 12 rows
Row 1 (RS): Using A, (sl1yo, brk1) 3 times, sl1yo, brRsldec, yo twice, sl1yo, brk1, sl1yo, yo twice, brLsldec, (sl1yo, brk1) 3 times. Do not turn, slide.
Row 2 (RS): Using B, (brp1, sl1yo) 4 times, (p1, sl1yo, brp1, sl1yo) twice, (brp1, sl1yo) 3 times. Turn.
Row 3 (WS): Using A, (brp1, sl1yo) to end. Do not turn, slide.
Row 4 (WS): Using B, (sl1yo, brk1) to end. Turn.
Row 5 (RS): Using A, (sl1yo, brk1) twice, sl1yo, brRsldec, yo twice, (sl1yo, brk1) 3 times, sl1yo, yo twice, brLsldec, (sl1yo, brk1) twice. Do not turn, slide.
Row 6 (RS): *(Brp1, sl1yo) 3 times, p1, sl1yo; rep from * once, (brp1, sl1yo) 3 times. Turn.
Rows 7 and 8 (WS): As rows 3 and 4.
Row 9 (RS): Using A, sl1yo, brk1, sl1yo, brRsldec, yo twice, (sl1yo, brk1) 5 times, sl1yo, yo twice, brLsldec, sl1yo, brk1. Do not turn, slide.
Row 10 (RS): Using B, (brp1, sl1yo) twice, p1, sl1yo, (brp1, sl1yo) 5 times, p1, sl1yo, (brp1, sl1yo) twice. Turn.
Rows 11 and 12 (WS): As rows 3 and 4.

SHAWL
Using A, cast on 8 sts.
SET-UP
Row 1 (RS): K2, (sl1yo, k1) 3 times.
Row 2 (WS): Sl1p, (brp1, sl1yo) 3 times, sl1p.
Row 3 (RS): K1, brkyobrk, sl1yo, br4stinc, sl1yo, brkyobrk, sl1yo, k1. Do not turn, slide sts back to other end of needle to work RS again (16 sts).
Row 4 (RS): Using B, sl1p, sl1yo, p1, sl1yo, brp1, sl1yo, p1, pm, sl1yo, p1, sl1yo, brp1, sl1yo, p1, sl1yo, brp1, sl1p. Turn.
Row 5 (WS): Using A, p1, (sl1yo, brp1) to last st, p1. Do not turn, slide.

Row 6 (WS): Using B, sl1p, (brk1, sl1yo) to last st, sl1p. Turn.
SECTION 1
Row 1 (RS): Using A, k1, brkyobrk, (sl1yo, brk1) to 1 st before m, sl1yo, sm, br4stinc, (sl1yo, brk1) to last 3 sts, brkyobrk, sl1yo, k1 (inc 8).
Do not turn, slide.
Row 2 (RS): Using B, sl1p, sl1yo, p1, (sl1yo, brp1) to m, remove m, sl1yo, p1, pm, sl1yo, p1, (sl1yo, brp1) to last 5 sts, sl1yo, p1, sl1yo, brp1, sl1p. Turn.
Row 3 (WS): Using A, p1, (sl1yo, brp1) to last st, p1. Do not turn, slide.
Row 4 (WS): Using B, sl1p, (brk1, sl1yo) to last st, sl1p. Turn.
Rep Section 1 once more (32 sts).
SECTION 2
Rows 1–3: As rows 1–3 of Section 1
Row 4 (WS): Using B, sl1p, brLsldec, (brk1, sl1yo) to last 5 sts, brRsldec, sl1yo, sl1 (dec 4).
Rep Section 2 two more times (44 sts). Cont as set, working Section 1 three times then Section 2 three times (inc 36 in each rep) until you have 320 sts: 1 edge st, 158 sts in two-colour brioche rib for first wing, 2 spine sts, 158 sts in two-colour brioche rib for second wing, 1 edge st.

SET BRIOCHE LACE PATT
Row 1 (RS): Using A, k1, brkyobrk, pm. Work Brioche Lace Patt 7 times, pm, sl1yo, brk1, sl1yo, sm, br4stinc, brk1, pm, work Brioche Lace Patt 7 times, pm, sl1yo, brkyobrk, sl1yo, k1. Cont working Sections 1 and 2 as set, but working Brioche Lace Patt between markers until you have worked 1 full patt rep.
Note: If your first Brioche Lace Patt row falls in Section 2, you will need to stop working the Brioche Lace Patt 1st before the last marker in order to work the decrease on row 4, which goes over 5 sts.
Work rows 1–4 of Section 1 again. Break B.
Using A, cast off using a stretchy cast off as foll: K1, *brk1, slip both sts back to LH needle and k2tog tbl, p1, slip sts back to LH needle and p2tog; rep from * to last st, k1, sl st back to LH needle and k2tog tbl, fasten off.

TO FINISH
Weave in ends (see page 71). Block gently to open out brioche lace pattern (see page 23).

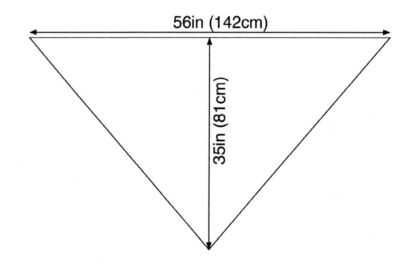

56in (142cm)

35in (81cm)

To order a book, contact:

GMC Publications Ltd,
Castle Place,
166 High Street,
Lewes, East Sussex,
BN7 1XU, United Kingdom
Tel: +44 (0)1273 488005
www.gmcbooks.com

CRAFTING **PERFECTION**

Countless reams have been written on the subject of overcoming perfectionism.
But how would it be if, just once in a while, we could create something that really is perfect?

Perfectionism gets a bad rap.

It has been called a 'hidden epidemic', has been the subject of countless self-help books and has been linked to mental health issues, such as obsessive-compulsive disorder, anxiety, body dysmorphia, depression and suicide.

I never considered myself a perfectionist until I heard it described as a general internal dissatisfaction, a feeling that one's work or oneself just wasn't quite up to par. In fact, I felt that my work and I myself were so far below even average standards that if I were to claim perfectionism I would give it a bad name. Real perfectionists (and probably everyone else) would laugh at me and point out that with my failings there was no way I could be one. I came to harbour a resentful sense of inadequacy towards genuine perfectionists, as if they belonged to a club I wasn't invited to join, or were in the beautiful garden Alice spies through the tiny door in Wonderland – wonderful but impossible to reach.

Apparently, this kind of feeling is rather typical of perfectionists.

But humans aren't perfect – we are bundles of flaws and imperfections, which is why artists throughout the ages have woven deliberate mistakes into their work for one reason or another. It is said that the Muslim weavers of Persian carpets always put in one deliberate flaw because only God's creation is perfect. In Fishbourne Roman Villa in West Sussex, UK, the famous Cupid mosaic has at least 28 deliberate mistakes, but no one knows why – curators suggest it may have been as a conversation piece, or even a design decision. In Navajo culture, rug weavers would leave little imperfections along the borders in the shape of a line, known as the 'spirit line' or 'spirit pathway'. According to the website amusingplanet.com, Navajos believe that when weaving a rug, weavers entwine parts of their beings into the cloth. The spirit line allows this trapped part of the weaver's spirit to safely exit the finished rug.

Whether perfectionism is a dangerous gateway into mental illness or a glorious Nirvana that may or may not be attainable, there is an obvious attraction to the idea of getting something – maybe just one thing – perfectly right.

It is not something I experienced myself until I took up knitting. Or rather, until I had been knitting on a regular basis for well over 30 years and could do it (on occasion) without looking, while watching TV. For many years I was what is known as a 'product knitter'. I bought yarn and patterns and churned out projects that I wanted to get done, because I wanted to wear them or show them off or give them to people as gifts. I often did this in a tearing hurry.

Only in the past few years have I, somewhat mysteriously, made the transition to being a 'process knitter'. I don't really know what changed, but now I love nothing more than the knitting itself, and sometimes even lose interest in projects after I've cast them off. At any time I might have two or three nearly, but not quite, finished projects lying around, because I'm having too much fun with a knit I'm in the middle of to bother getting them completely done.

All this may not sound very perfectionist to you. Don't worry, I'm coming to it.

As my interest in actually knitting overwhelmed my interest in producing a finished garment, I became less and less tolerant of mistakes. In the past, if I spotted a flaw a few rows back – or even, heaven forbid, right at the start of the knit – I would usually decide I could live with it, or fix it as an afterthought, or somehow fudge it so it wouldn't spoil the design. The breakthrough came when I was working on a super-quick project with a very thick, soft, gloriously expensive wool. The first attempt didn't turn out quite how I wanted it – so I undid it and started all over again. It was a treat, because it meant I had longer working with that particularly wool before the project was finished. The second attempt had a different problem. There was something wrong with the third. In the end I had to sit myself down in front of the TV and watch two films back to back so I could cast off the project before I got up again – if I hadn't forced myself to do that I might still be knitting and re-knitting the same blanket today.

It doesn't happen every time, but more and more I find that when I spot a mistake in my knitting, instead of that horrible sinking feeling, there is a sense of slightly naughty glee. More knitting for me! And that opens the door to perfection. If you can do something over and over, without a deadline, you could just keep doing it until it's exactly how you want it. Knitting particularly lends itself to this – if your knitting isn't OK you can just pull out the needles, unravel it and you'll end up with the wool in more or less the same state it started out in. (WARNING: This isn't true of every yarn – some do not unravel well, so be extra careful with those.) Even if you have cut it in places it's not really an issue, as it often involves using several different lengths of yarn anyway. The process would be considerably more complicated, for example, if you were sewing and had cut your fabric to the wrong shape.

Creating something you think is perfect gives you a sense of accomplishment and control – and, of course, perfectionism is all about control. As humans, we need to understand and accept that we live in a chaotic and unpredictable world where too often matters are simply beyond our influence. When we try too hard to impose order on ourselves and our circumstances – and more often than not fail to do so, and then feel bad about it – that is when the desire for perfection becomes a problem.

But just because perfectionism can be a problem doesn't mean it is something that has to be overcome. Or perhaps allowing ourselves something utterly perfect once in a while is part of overcoming perfectionism, and will help us to accept all the imperfect things that surround us. This piece of knitting is perfect; my waistline is not. This macramé plant holder is perfect; my performance at work is not. This decoupage project is perfect; unfortunately my home is now a total mess. I haven't got anyone to hang out with tonight; but look, I've just made this fabulous necklace – and it's perfect.

When you find a hobby you love, there are many wonderful things about it. Buying supplies, doing research, planning projects, starting out, working through, finishing and, finally, using or giving away the created item are all part of the pleasure of crafting. Having the power to create something that is perfect can lead to a real sense of accomplishment and even relief. Perhaps it is the relief of the perfectionist part of you feeling perfectly satisfied, just for once – just until the next time.

ABBREVIATIONS

alt	alternative
beg	begin/ning
brk1	brioche knit 1: knit together the slipped stitch from the previous row with the yarn over across it
brp1	brioche purl 1: purl together the slipped stitch from the previous row with the yarn over across it
cm	centimetre/s
cn	cable needle
cont	continue
dec	decrease
dpn(s)	double-pointed needle(s)
foll	follows/following
g	gramme/s
g st	garter stitch (every row knit)
in	inch/es
inc	increase
k	knit
k2tog	knit two stitches together (decrease 1)
k3tog	knit three stitches together (decrease 2)
kfb	knit into front and back of next stitch (increase 1)
kwise	knitwise
kyok	k1, yarn over, k1 all into the same stitch (inc 3)
LH	left hand
m	marker
m1	make 1 stitch: pick up the loop lying between the two stitches and knit into the back of it (increase 1)
m1L	use the LH needle to pick up the bar before the next st from front to back, then knit into the back of it
m1R	use the LH needle to pick up the bar before the next st from back to front, then knit it
m1p	make 1 purlwise
meas	measure/s
mm	millimetre/s
p	purl
p2tog	purl two stitches together (decrease 1)
p3tog	purl three stitches together (decrease 2)
patt	pattern
pm	place marker
psso	pass slipped stitch over
pwise	purlwise
rm	remove marker
rem	remain/ing
rep	repeat
rev st st	reverse stocking stitch (RS purl, WS knit)
RH	right hand
rnd	round
RS	right side
skpo	slip one, knit one, pass the slipped stitch over (decrease 1)
sk2po	slip one, knit two together, pass slipped stitch over (decrease 2)
s2kpo	slip two stitches one at a time knitwise, knit one, pass two slipped stitches over (decrease 2)
sp2po	slip one purlwise, purl two together, pass slipped stitch over (decrease 2)
sl1	slip one stitch
sl1p	slip one stitch purlwise
sl1yo	bring yarn to the front, slip next st pwise, work following stitch as directed creating a yarn over across the slipped stitch
sm	slip marker
ssk	slip next two stitches one at a time knitwise to right-hand needle, insert tip of left-hand needle through both stitches and knit them together (decrease 1)
st(s)	stitch(es)
st st	stocking stitch
tbl	through back loop
tog	together
WS	wrong side
wyib	with yarn at the back
wyif	with yarn at the front
yf	yarn forward
yo	yarn over

CONVERSIONS

The patterns in this book use UK knitting terms. Below are some translations for crafters who might be more familiar with US terms, which are sometimes different. We also include conversion tables for knitting needle sizes.

KNITTING NEEDLE SIZES

METRIC	UK	US
3.5mm	9	4
4mm	8	6
4.5mm	7	7
5mm	6	8
5.5mm	5	9
6mm	4	10
6.5mm	3	10½
8mm	0	1
10mm	000	15
12mm	–	17

KNITTING TERMS

UK	US
cast off	bind off
moss stitch	seed stitch
stocking stitch	stockinette stitch

SUPPLIERS

Cascade Yarns
cascadeyarns.com

Daughter of a Shepherd
daughterofashepherd.com

Debbie Bliss
lovecrafts.com

Erika Knight
erikaknight.co.uk

It's a Stitch Up
itsastitchup.co.uk

John Arbon
jarbon.com

Malabrigo
malabrigoyarn.com

Orchidean Luxury Yarns
luxuryyarns.co.uk

Rauwerk
rauwerk-wolle.de

Rico
rico-design.com

Rowan
knitrowan.com

The Wool Kitchen
thewoolkitchen.com

Tribe Yarns
tribeyarns.com

Triskelion Yarn
triskelion-yarn.com

Uist Wool
uistwool.com

We Are Knitters
weareknitters.co.uk

West Green Loft Yarns
westgreenloftyarns.com

West Yorkshire Spinners
wyspinners.com

Wool and the Gang
woolandthegang.com

ACKNOWLEDGEMENTS

Big thanks to the wonderfully supportive spinners and amazing yarn dyers who have backed this project. I love knitting with your yarns and really hope this book will lead others to do the same. This project wouldn't have been possible without the brilliant brain of pattern checker extraordinaire, actor, quizmaster and dressing-up queen Rachel Vowles, the vision, creativity and mindblowing efficiency of star designer Claire Stevens or the help of my amazing, super-talented former assistant Sophie Axtell. Thanks also to my employers at GMC, who have been flexible and supportive throughout. Thanks for support, inspiration and help from my knitting friends Pat Strong (who jumped in to knit two of the projects in this book when I was about to miss my deadline), Jo Allport, James McIntosh (knitnibble.com, knitmcintosh.com) and Sarah Hazell. Thanks to the brilliant team of photographer Laurel Guilfoyle (laurel-guilfoyle.co.uk) and gorgeous model Michiel Mhangami for a weird but beautiful lockdown photo shoot. On a personal note, I couldn't have done this (or made it through lockdown alive) without the constant cuddles, shrieking, emotional dramatics, crazy love and cups of tea and professional-quality coffee provided by my children Stanley and Daisy and my wonderful husband Glen, or the real-life and virtual support of my lovely friends, especially Juliet, Emma and Charly.

First published 2021 by
Guild of Master Craftsman Publications Ltd
Castle Place, 166 High Street, Lewes,
East Sussex BN7 1XU

ISBN 978 1 78494 584 8

A catalogue record for this book is available from the
British Library.

Publisher Jonathan Bailey
Production Manager Jim Bulley
Senior Project Editor Dominique Page
Designer Claire Stevens
Illustrator Rachel Vowles

Colour origination by GMC Reprographics
Printed and bound in China

Picture Credits
Photographs by Laurel Guilfoyle, except for on the
following pages: Anthony Bailey: 16, 18–22, 26–27, 30–32,
36, 70–71, 77 (bottom); Christine Boggis: 17, 23, 33, 37–39,
47, 50–51, 63–64, 76, 77 (top), 104–105, 120–121, 138–141;
Shutterstock.com: 10, 14, 48–49, 69, 97, 126–127, 146.